NO MAN LEFT BEHIND

CATHOLIC EDITION

NO MAN LEFT BEHIND

CATHOLIC EDITION

How to Build a Strong Disciple-Making Ministry for Every Man in Your Parish

CENTRAL TEXAS FELLOWSHIP
OF CATHOLIC MEN

Published by Wellspring

ISBN: 978-1-929266-73-9

Design by Ashley Wirfel

Library of Congress Cataloging-in-Publication Data
Names: National Fellowship of Catholic Men, author.
Title: No man left behind, Catholic edition / The National Fellowship of Catholic Men.
Description: North Palm Beach, Florida : Beacon Publishing, [2017]
Identifiers: LCCN 2017013251 | ISBN 9781929266739 (softcover : alk. paper)
Subjects: LCSH: Church work with men—Catholic Church. | Discipling (Christianity) | Spiritual formation.
Classification: LCC BV4440 .N6 2017 | DDC 259.0811—dc23

For more information on bulk copies of this title or other books and CDs available through the Dynamic Catholic Book Program, please visit www.DynamicCatholic.com or call 859-980-7900.

The Dynamic Catholic Institute
5081 Olympic Blvd • Erlanger • Kentucky • 41018
Phone: 1–859–980–7900
Email: info@DynamicCatholic.com

10 9 8 7 6 5 4 3 2

Printed in the United States of America

CONTENTS

ACKNOWLEDGMENTS

GOD WORKS in mysterious ways. I read a book called *Man in the Mirror* by Patrick Morley over ten years ago, and it had a dramatic impact on my life. Since then I have had the opportunity to get to know Patrick and his team at Man in the Mirror. Patrick Morley, David Delk, and Brett Clemmer wrote a book called *No Man Left Behind,* which is actually a playbook on ministry to men. After going through the No Man Left Behind training I realized we needed to take this book and introduce it to our Catholic brothers.

Patrick, David, and Brett helped us create *No Man Left Behind—Catholic Edition*. I cannot thank them enough for their support on this project. There are several other people who worked on this project for many years. Maurice Blumberg, the former executive director of the National Fellowship of Catholic Men, did a lot of the necessary rewriting and helped with Man in the Mirror. Maurice, thank you very much for all that you have done for Catholic men's ministry. Deacon Rae Carter in Waco, Texas, was also involved in the rewriting and has been an inspiration in my life. Thank you, Deacon Rae. Thomas Hibbs, dean of the Honors College at Baylor University, spent part of his summer in 2008 reviewing the book. Thank you for your input, Tom. This would not have been possible if it weren't for the support of the board of the National Fellowship of Catholic Men and its past executive director, Bill Moyer. Bill also was involved with the editing of the project.

I'd also like to thank a core team of Catholic men who came together to finalize the *No Man Left Behind—Catholic Edition* book project. Deacon Vincent Eberling did a great job of adding Roman Catholic thought, references, and footnotes. Dan Spencer, the current executive director of the National Fellowship of Catholic Men, added valuable insight to the project, and Mark Bruckbauer assisted with proofreading and commentary throughout the project. I want to thank each and every one of you for your prayers and for all your work on this project.

Robert E. Tunmire
Waco, Texas
September 21, 2015

PREFACE

And though a man might prevail against one who is alone, two will withstand him. A threefold cord is not quickly broken.
Ecclesiastes 4:12

THE ROMAN CATHOLIC CHURCH has a dire need for men to become saints. Before you close this book and set it aside because you do not believe you can become a saint, I ask you to stay with me for just a little longer.

We often hear the statistics of how the Catholic Church is in decline today. Certainly numbers of priests and religious have declined over the last few decades, especially in the Western Church; however, other parts of the world are in growth mode when it comes to converts to the faith.

It is my belief that the Roman Catholic Church will be re-energized when Catholic men decide and take action to become saints just as our Lord Jesus Christ invites us to become. The early Church's model for making saints and transforming the world was simple and yet powerfully effective. It consisted of small groups of ordinary, flawed humans who had a desire to seek God. The body of Christ, the Church, by the indwelling of the Holy Spirit, changed the world.

Jesus invites each man today on that same fantastic adventure. He invites each of us to be changed into men of holiness, men of action, men who lead our troubled world into a place of understanding, mercy, and peace.

This book aims to increase your share in the gifts of the Holy Spirit. It is a guidebook for starting, growing, and sustaining Catholic men's groups. *No Man Left Behind—Catholic Edition* is adapted and revised from the book *No Man Left Behind* written by three committed Christian men's ministry leaders: Dr. Patrick Morley, David Delk, and Brett Clemmer. These men lead a successful men's discipleship ministry called Man in the Mirror based in Orlando, Florida.

No Man Left Behind—Catholic Edition protects the integrity of the sustainability model which was shared in *No Man Left Behind* while incorporating Roman Catholic sacramental life and beliefs into the text. This book will enable Catholic men to approach their pastors in confidence about launching and developing Catholic men's groups. These groups will strengthen and renew Catholic men, who in turn will evangelize the Catholic Church in the United States.

May our Lord lead us to become the leaders and saints that is our birthright as Catholic men so that our spouses, our families, our parishes, and our communities may experience the light of the world which is Jesus Christ. Mary, our mother, pray for us.

INTRODUCTION

NO MAN LEFT BEHIND—CATHOLIC EDITION comes from a close partnership between the National Fellowship of Catholic Men and Man in the Mirror ministries. Both national organizations have a passion for forming men as disciples. The original book, *No Man Left Behind,* has been used by Protestants and Catholics alike, but the book terminology is primarily that used in Evangelical Protestant churches. This book has been designed to resonate with Catholic men and includes Catholic terminology, concepts, and teachings.

We believe nothing has the power to transform the world more than forming men as disciples. We've seen it in parishes where pastors and men's leaders passionately commit to reach all of their men. It's not easy, but it's among a handful of the most important tasks in the world. How important for Catholics is this call to discipleship? Consider these words from a United States Conference of Catholic Bishops (USCCB) document:

> Christian faith is lived in discipleship to Jesus Christ. As disciples, through the power of the Holy Spirit, our lives become increasingly centered on Jesus and the kingdom he proclaims. By opening ourselves to him we find community with all his faith-filled disciples and by their example come to know Jesus more intimately. By following the example of his self-giving love we learn to be Christian disciples in our own time, place, and circumstances.
>
> God's call to conversion and discipleship unfolds in our lives with immeasurable potential for maturing and bearing fruit. The calls to holiness, to community, and to service of God and neighbor are "facets of Christian life that come to full expression only by means of development and growth toward Christian maturity."[1]

We believe God is moving powerfully among Catholic men. Listen to what the USCCB had to say about this move of God in its *Catholic Men's Ministries* report:

> From Los Angeles to Chicago, from Manchester to Miami, there is a growing hunger for God among Catholic men. They are meeting together in large and small groups, sharing their burdens, listening to each other's story, and celebrating Eucharist. Call it a revival, an awakening. Call it a work of the Holy Spirit at the grassroots level. The emergence of new ministries with men is a welcome development in the Church.[2]

In light of what is going on today in the world and in our culture, now more than ever do the Church, Catholic families, and our country need strong Catholic men standing shoulder to shoulder. It seems clear that we can't fight and overcome evil on our own by being lone ranger Christians.

The goal of the National Fellowship of Catholic Men is to have Catholic men's conferences in all two hundred dioceses in the United States, to have men's fellowship groups in each of the 17,000 U.S. parishes, and to provide support, training, and resources to help bring all of this about. With over fifty-five Catholic men's conferences conducted in 2008 and a significant increase in parish-based men's groups, this goal does not seem as daunting as it once did. Tens of thousands of Catholic men are being touched by God through Catholic men's conferences and the thousands of parish-based men's groups supported by the National Fellowship of Catholic Men.

This is great news, but the issue remains: How do we successfully sustain this initial work of God in Catholic men so that they become mature Christian disciples of Jesus Christ? We believe that an important element is having a well-defined approach for forming Catholic men as disciples. On page ten of this book is an image of the No Man Left Behind Model. We'll explain this system throughout the book, and our hope is that by the end you will be able to pass the "napkin test," which means you'll be able to explain this system in a few minutes to another man using nothing but a pen and a paper napkin.

This book largely represents what Man in the Mirror has learned in a combined eighty years of experience forming men as disciples, and almost thirty years of working with pastors and church leaders who are doing the same. Man in the Mirror has worked with both Catholic and Protestant churches (from more than one hundred denominations), and it has partnerships with more than a dozen denominations. It has worked very closely with the National Fellowship of Catholic Men (NFCM) in supporting its vision, "Catholic Men, Linked as Brothers in Jesus Christ, and Called to Bring Him to Others." It has conducted more than fifty classes in men's discipleship through its Leadership Training Center. It has worked directly with pastors and the leadership teams of more than 2,500 churches, and has had the opportunity to learn from thousands more. It has conducted extensive research and fieldwork in hundreds of churches. We believe God has given Man in the Mirror these unique opportunities in large measure so that we could write this book.

This is our life's work. Helping pastors and church leaders disciple men is what we do. We have the privilege of waking up every day focused on how to disciple men in the Church—your church. We will be honored if God uses this book to make your efforts to disciple Catholic men more effective and your path a little easier.

Unless otherwise noted, the stories in this book are true (though names are often disguised, and for the purpose of making the book resonate with Catholic readers, some Catholic details have been added). These are real churches and real men with real stories. Each chapter also contains discussion questions and exercises. It will be best if you do these as a men's ministry leadership team or with another man from your parish. The first chapter gives you a helicopter view of the book. The final chapter ties all your work together and helps you outline concrete next steps to more effectively disciple the men of your parish.

Thanks for making the investment in this book and in the men in your parish. We want to be involved with you and help however we can. We also want to keep learning. If you have questions or feedback, please email us at the National Fellowship of Catholic Men (info@nfcmusa.org), or Man in the Mirror (nomanleftbehind@maninthemirror.org).

God, as we start this journey, we commit ourselves to you. Help us be faithful. Make us passionate for you and for our Catholic men. Give us the insights and strategies we need to raise up an army of Catholic men who will fight for your kingdom and glory. In the powerful name of Jesus, Amen.

The NO MAN LEFT BEHIND Model

A System Designed to Produce Passionate Disciples

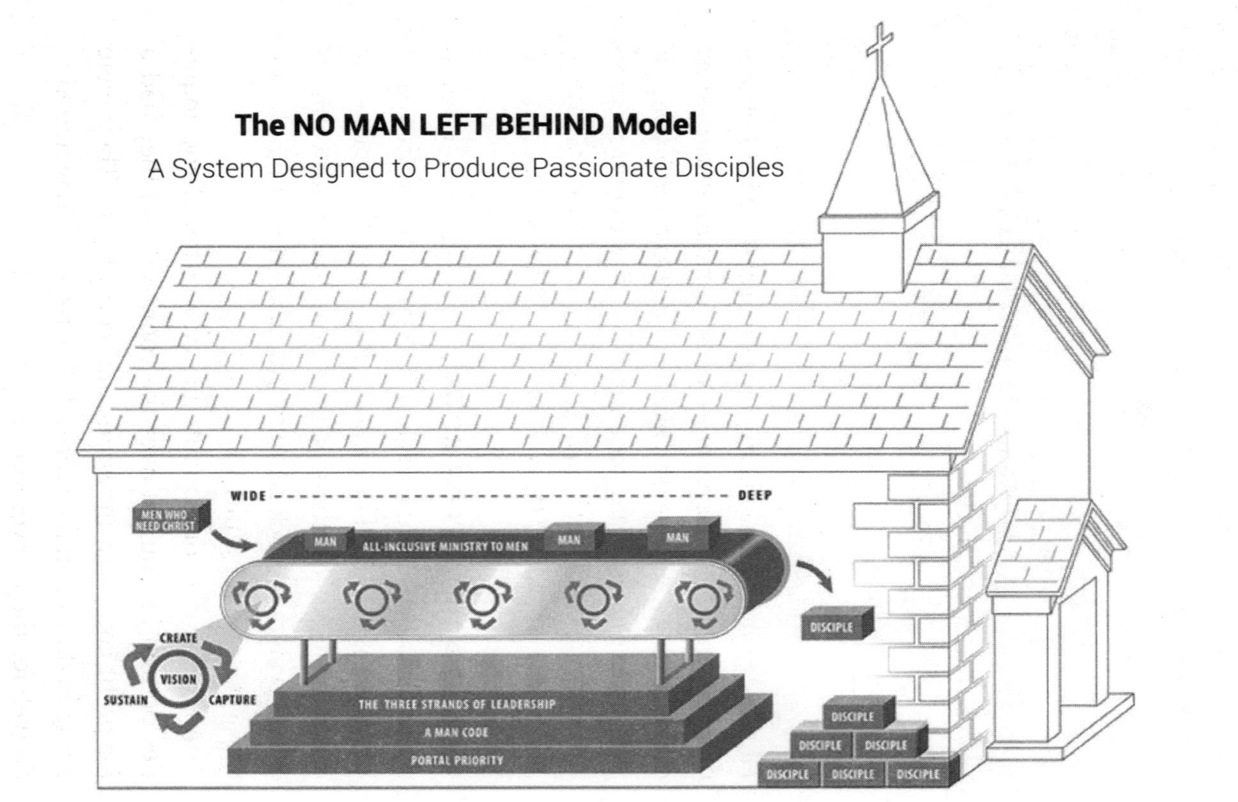

1

MEN'S MINISTRY IS ROCKET SCIENCE

Pat Morley, one of the authors of the original No Man Left Behind *book, has a favorite business saying he picked up somewhere along the way: "Anyone can bring me a problem; I'm looking for people who can also bring me a solution." This chapter provides an overview of a proven system to help you disciple every man in your parish. The rest of the book will unpack this system in detail.*

DURING A HIGH-TECH BOOM, a few young professionals in Orlando, Florida, decided to start a dream company. With backgrounds in helping the homeless, the jobless, the disadvantaged, and the sick, they created a unique computerized system to track cases as they passed through the social services community.

As word got out about this new technology, inquiries poured in from all over the country. Soon they had a for-profit company, investors, and consultants. They were going to do well in the world. In the process, they hoped to do well for themselves too.

THE AMERICAN DREAM

One of those young professionals was responsible for selling the company's software. In its first year, the business made its first million dollars in sales. It was hard work. This salesman would go anywhere, anytime, to talk to anybody. He attended countless conferences and made dozens of sales presentations. He was living the American Dream: being in on the ground floor of a technology company.

Soon, venture capitalists started calling. They told him and his team how they should grow. They said if certain benchmarks were hit, they would be ready to invest. He and his team began to believe they would hit it big.

Following the venture capitalists' advice, he hired a national sales force. Soon six people scattered across the country were looking for potential customers. But those salespeople were new to both social services and the technology, so after they found the prospects, he flew out to make the presentations. Instead of one person scheduling trips for him, he now had six people doing it!

THE BUBBLE BURSTS

Then the stock market started to go south. Suddenly the venture capitalists that had been breathlessly waiting for the company to grow stopped returning phone calls—even as the team met the potential investors' benchmarks.

"When the going gets tough, the tough get going," this salesman had heard all his life. So he worked even harder. Even without the capital from those investors, he was determined to make the company a success through sheer will.

One afternoon, he got an excited call from his representative in Texas. He asked him to come the next day to meet with a large government prospect. A little weary, the salesman called his wife to break the news that he had to go on yet another trip, and on short notice. Her response caught him off guard. "That's OK," she said. "It's easier when you're not here."

He tried to laugh it off. "Easier when I'm not there. Ha!" The man and his wife had two small children, were active in their church, and owned a home. What was she talking about? When he got home, he asked her.

"I mean it's easier when you're not here," she repeated. "You're trying to build a company, I understand. But it's not easy for me either. You call at five thirty to say you're finishing up and you'll be home in thirty minutes, then you walk in at eight o' clock. I try to keep dinner warm, but it's ruined. I'm the one who has to answer the kids when they ask, 'Where's Daddy?' or 'Why is Daddy so grumpy?' When you are here, you're so tired that you pretty much ignore us. So go on your trip. We'll be fine. Really. It's just easier when you're not here."

He was in trouble. Worst of all, he didn't really know how it happened. He had told himself he was doing it all for his family. He would buy a nice house in a good neighborhood for his wife, send his kids to good schools, and give money to charity. But somewhere along the line, he had lost his way. He realized it hadn't really been about his family; it had been about him.

Ironically, while he was losing himself in his company, he and his wife were busy at their church, where they led several hundred grade school children in the youth program.

He grew up in church, and now he was a leader in his present church. And yet his wife and family preferred for him to be gone. It was easier. He had become a distraction in their lives.

Why was he being left behind? Why hadn't he connected with his church in a way that helped him become a passionate disciple of Jesus Christ?

Does any of this story resonate with your life? How about some men that you know?

THE PARADOX OF MEN'S MINISTRY: IT REALLY IS ROCKET SCIENCE

Men's Ministry. How hard can it be? Think about it: You've got men; you've got a parish. Add a testimony, some pancakes, a prayer, and—poof!—a Catholic men's ministry. Or perhaps not, especially in light of these words of John Paul II to American bishops:

> Sometimes even Catholics have lost or never had the chance to experience Christ personally; not Christ as a mere "paradigm," but the Living Lord: "the way, the truth, and the life" (John 14:6).[3]

We've worked with thousands of Catholic and Protestant churches across America to help them disciple men. Leaders from parishes all over the world have journeyed to Orlando to attend classes at our Leadership Training Center. This book is based on what we've learned from these and other parishes. You get to stand on their shoulders.

To encourage and motivate these leaders, we used to tell

them: "Look, what we're trying to do here is not rocket science."

And then during one class . . . a new insight. As we stared at this group of leaders struggling to reach men in their parishes, we realized that these were not clueless men. Many were successful businessmen. They were accomplished, intelligent, hardworking men. And yet, year after year they were struggling to reach and disciple the men in their parishes.

Why? Because men's ministry is grueling. As one leader said, "A man is a hard thing to reach."

> Men's ministry actually is rocket science. While the process is simple enough, men themselves are quite complex.

When you are working on rockets, things are pretty objective. It's all about physical laws and mathematical concepts like gravity, velocity, angles of ascent, and coefficients of drag. But men are not nearly as predictable. Rockets don't get laid off, have trouble with their kids, or endure a health crisis.

Still, there are some parallels between rocket science and men's ministry. For example:

- ***Gravity.*** Most men shoulder the burden of supporting a family financially, trying to be a good husband and father, and resisting the temptations of a world that wants to drag them down.
- ***Velocity.*** Some Catholics, especially recently converted Catholics, go like gangbusters. But many men have been in their parish for a long time, their enthusiasm is waning, and they often end up simply attending Mass.

- ***Angles of ascent.*** Some men get it and steadily move forward; others careen back and forth in their spiritual journey, veering off and hurting people as they go. The key is to ensure they are moving toward Christlikeness.
- ***Coefficients of drag.*** Jobs, soccer games, family problems, parish commitments, hobbies. . . . All these seem to hold men back as they seek to develop or deepen their faith and their ministry.

If you've been struggling to get traction in your men's ministry, this should bring you relief and hope. It brings relief when you understand it's not just you (it really is hard to reach and disciple men), and hope because this book contains a strategy that can help you do it. You can reach men in your parish. You can get them to grow closer to Christ.

THE PHYSICS OF MEN'S MINISTRY

You must accept several constants, however, if you are going to launch and sustain a powerful men's ministry. (These will come up again later, but it's good to manage your expectations from the start.) Here are three realistic parameters to remember:

First, it takes a long time to make a disciple. Jesus spent three years with his disciples, traveling with them, eating with them, teaching them. Even then, one of them sold him out, another one denied he even knew him, and all of them panicked and hid after Jesus was killed. How can we expect to make disciples in a twenty-four-week class?

Second, it can take up to ten years to build and sustain a suc-

cessful men's ministry. That's right. Ten years. As Richard Foster said, "Our tendency is to overestimate what we can accomplish in one year, but underestimate what we can accomplish in ten years."[4] There's just no such thing as an "overnight men's ministry success story." If you stick with it, eventually you'll look around your parish and see men who are disciples and leaders. You'll realize that your ministry is responsible in some way for most of those men. And it will take ten years. You are not called to produce immediate results, just to be faithful.

Third, there are no "Five Easy Steps to an Effective Men's Ministry." There aren't even five *hard* steps. At the Leadership Training Center, they sometimes refer to this as "Insert Tab A into Slot B Men's Ministry." It just doesn't work that way. This book is *preceptive,* not *prescriptive.* It explains "why" and "how" to disciple men, but won't specify exactly "what" to do. Instead, it will help you plan your own concrete next steps according to the culture and needs of your parish.

FROM PROTOTYPE TO MANUFACTURING

The cold, hard reality is that we will not see a revival in America and the world if effective disciple-building of men does not move from the prototype stage to the manufacturing stage. What do we mean by that? Imagine you were alive in 1900. You might have seen an automobile drive through town. People would have gathered to point and stare at this unusual new apparatus. But only twenty-five years later, to see an automobile would have been no big deal. Why? In 1913 Henry Ford invented the assembly line with a conveyor belt. By 1927 the Ford Motor Company had manufactured fifteen million Model Ts! Ford helped move the auto industry from the prototype stage to the manufacturing stage.

The BIG Idea

The discipleship system of your church is perfectly designed to produce the kind of men you have sitting in the pews.

Right now, many Catholic parishes are doing a wonderful job of empowering men to become disciples using a variety of different programs. You may have heard about some of them. There are approximately 17,000 parishes in America, according to CARA's 2016 statistics.[5] Our passion is to see a dynamic disciple-making ministry to men in all these parishes. Forming men as disciples needs to move from an unusual activity in a few parishes to a common characteristic of parish life.

A PERFECTLY DESIGNED SYSTEM

What about your parish? In business we have an axiom: "Your system is perfectly designed to produce the results you are getting." Imagine a factory where the front right fender falls off every third car that rolls off the assembly line. The manufacturing "system" of the factory is perfectly designed to produce cars that have a one in three chance of a fender falling off!

This applies to more than manufacturing processes. The same can be said of ministry systems (or models). In other words, the discipleship "system" of your parish is perfectly designed to produce the kind of men you have sitting in the pews (or not sitting in the pews, as the case may be).

HOW THIS BOOK IS STRUCTURED

That's why in this book we focus on helping parishes and equipping and training leaders. We will present you with a system designed to sustain an effective disciple-making ministry to men in your parish. This model has already been proven in many churches—it's a system that works, a system that's designed to create passionate disciples.

The goal is to form Catholic men who embody the Great Commandment—to love God with their whole heart, mind, soul, and strength and to love their neighbor as themselves.

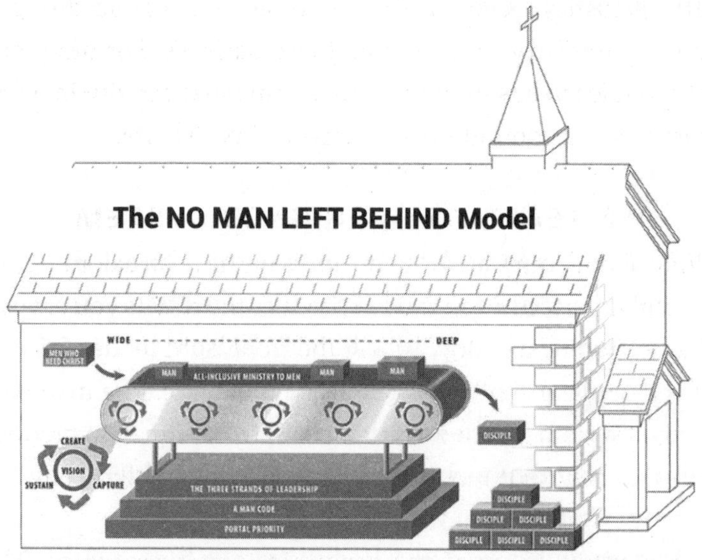

This model demonstrates how to build a "people mover" or "conveyor belt" to disciple men within your parish. Just like a moving sidewalk at an airport or an assembly line at Henry Ford's factory, this process helps men get from where they are to where God calls them to be.

The remainder of this chapter presents an overview of the components of the model as well as a preview of what's to come in the rest of the book. We'll take a helicopter view and fly over the major concepts and insights. Don't feel like you have to grasp it all now—the following chapters unpack each aspect step-by-step.

It's important to be familiar with all of these ideas before discussing each one in detail because together they form an integrated whole. This system is most definitely more than the sum of its parts.

The model has three sections. The purpose of "Part One: The Promise of Men's Ministry" is to better understand how men are doing, what they need, and how to help them. The purpose of "Part Two: The Foundations of Your Ministry to Men" is to understand the building blocks of a sustainable discipleship system in your parish. The purpose of "Part Three: Executing Your Men's Ministry" is to give you a strategy to disciple every man in your parish.

By the end of chapter twelve, especially if you work through it with a team, you will create a concrete plan for exactly what to do in your parish.

Part one will be explored in chapters two through four, part two in chapters five through seven, and part three in chapters eight through twelve. Here's a quick introduction to each.

PART 1: THE PROMISE OF MEN'S MINISTRY: WHAT YOUR PARISH CAN DO FOR MEN

Before you start building a system, it's a good idea to understand both your starting and ending points. We begin with the men. Exactly what is it we hope to accomplish with them?

The men you are trying to reach are the raw materials of your system. The men in your parish community are the inputs on the left side of the conveyor belt. You will read more about the state of men in America in chapter two.

Your goal is to create an environment that God can use to produce active, committed disciples. As we know, disciples are men who are called to walk with Christ (converted), equipped to live like Christ (formed), and sent to work for Christ (mobilized)—see 2 Timothy 2:15. They are the *outputs,* or products, of your men's ministry system; they are men who are mature in their Catholic faith.

The introduction to *Our Hearts Were Burning within Us: A Pastoral Plan for Adult Faith Formation in the United States* puts it this way:

> We are eager to witness and share the word of life about the reign of God faithfully, so that each new generation can hear this word in its own accents and discover Christ as its Savior. Every disciple of the Lord Jesus shares in this mission. To do their part, adult Catholics must be mature in faith and well equipped to share the gospel, promoting it in every family circle, in every parish gathering, in every place of work, and in every public forum. They must be women and men of prayer whose faith is alive and

> vital, grounded in a deep commitment to the person and message of Jesus.[6]

Some disciples will become leaders, and some of these leaders will become allies. What do men look like at each of these stages? Chapter three will cover leaders in depth, but below is an overview of the basic stages.

1. ***Mature Catholic Disciples.*** These are men who embrace a close relationship with the Lord and seek to live a godly life, characterized by faithful participation in Mass, regular reception of the sacraments (the Eucharist and Reconciliation are crucial—see *CCC*, 1324, 1422), and an active prayer life. They grasp the gospel and are hungry to grow. They have stopped seeking the God they want and have begun to seek the God who is. They understand that change takes place from the inside out. They know from their own experience that Christianity is not only about behavior modification; it's about the continual conversion that leads to spiritual transformation. The Catechism describes them as men who live into the fullness of their baptism (see *CCC*, 1227) and are sealed by the anointing of the Holy Spirit in confirmation (see *CCC*, 1289). We go into greater detail about mature, faith-filled Catholics in chapter nine.
2. ***Leaders.*** These are men who are beginning to live out of the overflow of their own personal relationship with the Lord Jesus. No longer are they concerned only with their walk with God; now they want to do what it takes to help other people grow too. These are the "trustworthy"

men who will, in turn, pass what they have learned on to others. Read more about leaders in chapter six.

3. ***Allies.*** These are men who have become passionately convinced that God can use them, and other men in your parish, to transform the world for His glory. These are the men who become future members of your men's leadership team and fuel growth in your discipleship ministry with men. Pray and focus your energies on creating allies. Read more about allies in chapter four.

PART 2: THE FOUNDATIONS OF YOUR MINISTRY TO MEN

Three components provide a solid base on which to build your men's ministry—the Portal Priority (your philosophy of ministry), a Man Code (the environment you create for men), and the Three Strands of Leadership.

The Portal Priority. Parishes that reach men effectively make discipleship their portal priority ("Go therefore and make disciples of all nations, baptizing them in the name of the Father and of the Son and of the Holy Spirit"). By this we mean that all the other initiatives of the parish serve the purpose of discipleship. You cannot produce worshipers by begging men to worship; you can't produce faithful stewards by shaming men to give; you can't create Catholic evangelists simply by training men to share. Men will not worship a God they do not know and revere; they won't give to a God they don't love; and they won't share about a God they aren't passionate about. Jesus' model is to produce disciples who worship; disciples who give generously of their time, talent, and treasure; and disciples who are passionate to share the good news about what He has done for them. We discuss the portal priority in chapter five.

A Man Code. Parishes that effectively disciple men have a strong masculine atmosphere. They create an unwritten "man code" that defines what it means to be a man in their parish. New men soak it in from the atmosphere: "To be a man here is to be important and valuable, and also to play a part in what God is doing to transform the world." Sometimes the incredible adventure of following Christ is buried beneath boring bulletin announcements. Many men are just waiting for an invitation. Make your parish a place where men can be men. You'll read more about a man code in chapter five.

The Three Strands of Leadership. To disciple all the men of your parish community, your conveyor belt will need a strong foundation, which comes from leadership. Successful discipleship ministries for men have the endorsement and involvement of the pastor (an ordained priest), a committed leader (which could be a priest or deacon but will most often be a layman), and an effective and renewed lay leadership team—three strands of leadership (like the cord of three strands in Ecclesiastes 4:12). Leadership is explored in chapter six.

ABOVE THE FOUNDATION: THE PROCESS

On top of this foundation, we will help you build a "conveyor belt" process of your men's ministry.

Wide to Deep. Parishes that reach men build a system that moves men along the "wide-to-deep" continuum. A goal of your parish men's ministry is to meet men who may be lukewarm in their faith (interested in opportunities on the wide side) and move them along toward becoming passionate disciples (invested in ministry on the deep side). Each activity or program in your parish will appeal to men who are at different points on the continuum. One role of leadership is to make sure all your leaders are on the same page and that you have the entire continuum covered to help disciple every man.

All-Inclusive. Develop an all-inclusive mind-set by recognizing that everything your parish does that touches men is men's ministry. In other words, the size of your men's ministry is equal to the number of men in your parish. The traditional understanding of men's ministry includes only those activities that happen when men are by themselves, such as Knights of Columbus meetings, Saturday morning men's communion breakfasts, or men's Bible studies. All-inclusive men's ministries disciple men right where they are, maximizing every interaction with every man. You have a "men's ministry" with every man in your parish—the only question is, "Is it effective?"

The wide-to-deep continuum and the all-inclusive ministry are both detailed in chapter seven.

PART 3: PLANNING AND EXECUTING YOUR MEN'S MINISTRY

Once the conveyor belt is built, you need an engine to start it in motion. You'll build and execute your plan with the *Vision-Create-Capture-Sustain* strategy. Implementing this strategy helps move men step-by-step along the continuum to become mature disciples. Here's a brief introduction to the elements, which

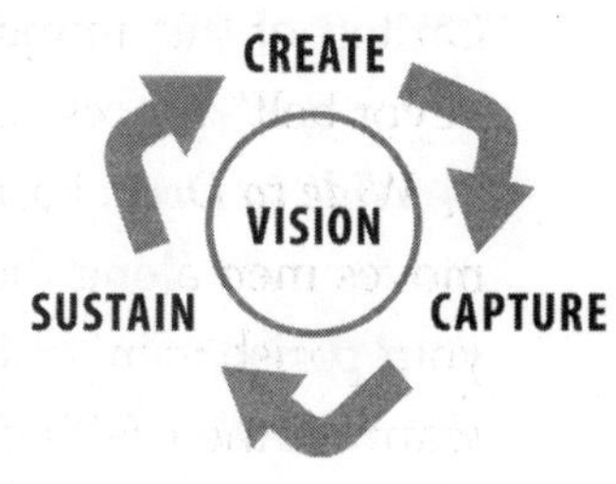

are described in detail in chapters eight through eleven, respectively.

Vision. Parishes that produce strong disciples clearly define and communicate their vision in ways that resonate with men. Use a name and a slogan or phrase that connect with men at a gut level. In every interaction you have with men, explain clearly and passionately how this event or activity helps fulfill your purpose and brings glory to God.

Create. *Create momentum* with men by creating value. Get a man started in discipleship by helping him take a new step spiritually. Invite him to breakfast, a men's group meeting, a men's Bible study, a Catholic men's conference, a retreat, or a special men's activity. If he says yes, it's because you have given him something he believes will be valuable.

Capture. *Capture momentum* by giving every man a "right next step" at the time that you create momentum. Use short-term, low-threshold activities that make it easy for a man to keep moving forward. For example, offer a six-week topical study on a commonly felt need, such as deepening our faith, or perhaps money (financial planning), or work.[7] Make sure you capture momentum by asking men for a commitment at the time they most feel the value.

Sustain. *Sustain momentum* by engaging men in the most effective long-term discipleship processes of your parish. As quickly as possible, help men enter into meaningful relationships with other men through small Catholic men's fellowship groups. Most lasting change takes place in the context of relationships. Sustain change by focusing on the heart rather than allowing men to simply be nice and perform.

Repeat this cycle over and over through your interactions

with men and see how God uses it to help men become passionate disciples.

Building Your Plan. This system will work differently in every parish. In chapter twelve, we walk through the entire model again step-by-step. We give you two sets of exercises—one to work through in the next three months, the other in the next year. This will give you a chance to build a concrete plan that fits your parish.

What is the result of implementing this system in a parish? You'll be a part of a dynamic parish filled with passionate men who live and love like Christ. We have seen this in hundreds of churches across America.

WHY IS THIS SO IMPORTANT?

Parishes dedicate a great deal of money and time each year to various programs. However, according to the Center for Applied Research in the Apostolate (CARA), associated with Georgetown University, only 24 percent of self-identified Catholics attend Mass on a weekly basis. One is tempted to ask, "What strides have been realized in areas like retention of Catholic men at Mass, divorce prevention, or fathering?" The consequences are staggering. Many from the baby boomer generation were raised by divorced or separated parents. Now the sins of the fathers are being visited on the next generation: Tonight, 33 percent of America's seventy-two million children will go to bed in a home without a biological father. Sixty-six percent of them are not expected to live with both biological parents through age eighteen.[8] We are now bearing the full brunt of the consequences of our failure to disciple men.

THE OPPORTUNITY: THE MAN COMES AROUND

The story at the beginning of this chapter is not an illustration. It's the true account of one of the authors of the original *No Man Left Behind* book, Brett Clemmer.

About the time his wife told him it was easier when he was gone, he got a call from a friend. "You know how our wives are meeting in that women's Bible study? Well, I was talking to some of the other husbands. Maybe we should have a guys' group too—if for no other reason than to protect ourselves, because I'm pretty sure they're talking about us." Brett was pretty sure too. He wondered what his friend had heard about *him*. "Sure," he said. "What are we going to study?"

"Remember the book they handed out a few weeks ago? Just bring that and we'll see if we want to use it."

He brought the book, and that group, he says, was the beginning of a rebirth of his faith:

> The book was *The Man in the Mirror*. We decided to study it, and it saved my marriage, my family, and in many ways, my life. The book spoke directly to what I was going through—the whole concept of cultural Christianity seemed like it was taken right from my experience.

He adds that the most important part of their study was the half-dozen guys he met—"all of us struggling to be good fathers and husbands, all working too hard and trying to find balance. It gave me brothers. And together, we journeyed toward Christ."

His software company eventually went out of business. "But a funny thing happened as my dream of building a company died," he said. "As my career plummeted, my relationship with my wife and my kids soared. And I found new life in my relationships with my brothers and with God." Why? Someone chose to call him to become a disciple.

You have men in your parish like this man. This book has been written to help you reach them and disciple them for their good and the glory of Christ. Thanks for joining the adventure. Together we can ask God to help us make sure that no Catholic man is left behind.

Remember This . . .

- Men's ministry actually is rocket science, only harder.
- It takes a long time to make a disciple.
- It can take up to ten years to build a successful men's ministry.
- There's no such thing as "The Five Easy Steps to an Effective Men's Ministry."
- Formation of men for discipleship needs to go from the prototype stage to the manufacturing stage (i.e., from conversion to transformation to mobilization for mission).
- Your system for building disciples is perfectly designed to produce the men who are sitting in your pews—or not.
- The No Man Left Behind Model will help you move men in your parish step-by-step toward becoming mature Catholic disciples.

Talk About This . . .

Discuss these questions with your leadership team:

1. "Men's ministry actually is rocket science." Do you agree or not, and why? What has been your past experience trying to build a men's ministry?
2. In a few sentences, how would you describe the "system" for reaching and forming men as disciples in your parish today? What kind of results have you been getting?
3. Look back at the No Man Left Behind Model. Which concepts are you looking forward to learning about, and why?

Pray About This . . .

Pray together as a leadership team:

- That God will unite your hearts as you seek to develop an effective discipleship ministry to men in your parish and in parishes throughout your diocese.
- That God will reveal how you can apply what you learn.
- That your parish will be a place where every man is discipled and no Catholic man is left behind, and that your diocese would be filled with parishes like yours.

PART ONE

THE PROMISE OF MEN'S MINISTRY

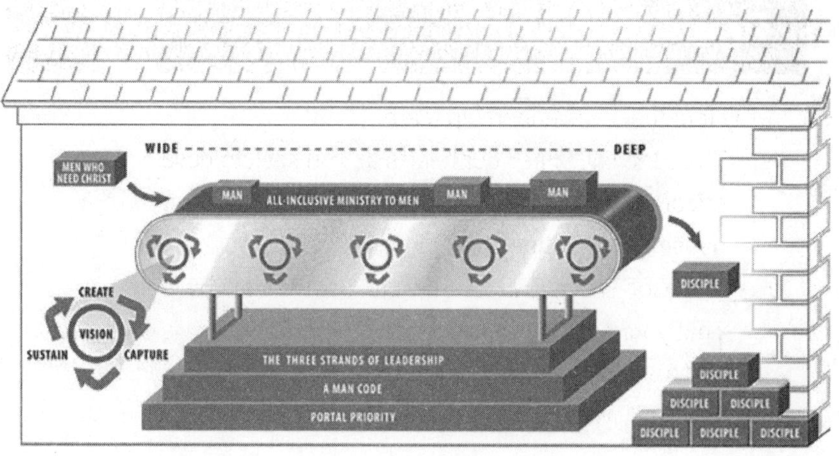

2
NO MAN FAILS ON PURPOSE

Before you can get the right answer, you have to ask the right question. What is the state of men in America today? And what difference does it make? When we see and understand the ramifications of men who are failing, we'll understand that starting with men is a systemic solution to the problems of our churches and the world.

MANY, IF NOT MOST, of our cultural problems—divorce, abortion, juvenile crime, fatherlessness—can be traced back to the failure of a man. Ironically, it's a man who got up in the morning hoping to succeed.

The signs are all around us. We live in a country where every third child is born out of wedlock; where

- **72,000,000** children under eighteen. Tonight, 33% of them will go to bed in a home without a biological father.
- **40%** of first marriages end in divorce, affecting one million children each year. Divorce rates for second and third marriages are higher.
- **33%** of all children are born out of wedlock.

SOURCES: U.S. Census Bureau; Wade F. Horn and Tom Sylvester, *Father Facts*, 4th ed.; (Gaithersburg, MD: National Fatherhood Initiative, 2002); and James Dobson, *Bringing Up Boys* (Wheaton: Tyndale, 2001).

twenty-four million kids don't live with their biological fathers; where about half of all marriages end in divorce. We can read these statistics and just blow by them. Or we can consider what they mean for our country and our churches. Wouldn't you agree that there must be something systemically wrong with a culture that allows these things to happen?

Fatherlessness is a rampant and well-documented problem in our society. Only a third of all children in America will live with both of their biological parents through the age of eighteen. Half of all children in broken homes have not seen their father in over a year. Children who come from fatherless homes are five times more likely to live in poverty, have emotional problems, and repeat a grade.

Yet, these are all symptoms of deeper systemic issues. Treating symptoms is necessary and good, but you can't cure a disease by treating the symptoms. So while there are many sociological and psychological studies to explain why we have so many problems, the "root" problem—the systemic problem—is that we have not properly discipled our men. The only way to solve systemic problems is with systemic solutions.

BABIES IN THE RIVER

In social service circles, a parable is told about a small village on the edge of a river. One day one of the villagers noticed a baby floating in the water. The villager quickly swam out to save the baby and brought it to shore.

The next day another villager was walking beside the river and saw two babies in the river. He quickly jumped in the water and rescued them. The following day four babies were rescued by the villagers. Every day the number of children in the water increased.

The villagers organized themselves quickly, building piers, tying rope lines, and training teams to rescue babies. They were soon working day and night. And still the number of children floating down the river increased each day.

The villagers worked as hard as they could, even to the point of exhaustion. But no one ever asked the question, "Why are these babies in the river? Let's go upstream and see where they are coming from."

What is the upstream cause of our cultural and spiritual ills? Consider a concrete issue like divorce. You sometimes hear a story about a wife who had an affair and left her husband, or a child whose behavior is so bad it rips the family apart. But you only hear about these stories because they are relatively rare. And often, even if a wife does have an affair, it's only after years of emotional neglect—if not abuse—by a husband *who was never taught what it takes to have a successful marriage.*

Although the Catholic divorce rate is lower than the U.S. average, it is still a daunting figure. It is important to remember that the percentage represents more than eleven million individuals. Most are likely in need of more outreach and ongoing ministry from the Church.[9]

Now let's consider teen pregnancy: Young men who have had the proper values instilled in them by their father will know how to treat young women. Young women who are secure in the love of their father and of God won't look for acceptance in the arms of young men. Do the men in your parish know how to teach their teenagers about sex, chastity, and God's plan for them to find happiness in a loving marriage relationship?

How about crime? Men comprise 93 percent of the prison population in America. And of those, 85 percent report having no father figure in their lives. How many of those men would be in jail right now if their fathers had stuck around and been involved in their lives?[10]

No one is trying to beat up on men here. If anything, we're saying: "Look how important men are! Look what happens when they aren't taught to do the right things!"

BUT IT'S BETTER IN THE CHURCH, RIGHT?

You'd think the Church would be a safe haven from many of these disturbing statistics. Surely kids who grow up going to church will have a foundation of faith that carries into adulthood. If a couple goes to church together, you would think that their marriage will be much more likely to succeed. Unfortunately, neither of these assumptions is true.

In fact, men in the Church face the same challenges and frustrations as men outside of the Church. For example, for every ten men in the Church:

- Nine will have children who leave the Church.[11]
- Eight will not find their jobs satisfying.[12]
- Six will watch porn at least once a month.[13]
- All ten will struggle to balance work and family.

Ask pastors to list the problems and struggles their members face. They sound like the chapter headings in a social work textbook: alcohol and substance abuse, pornography, domestic violence, juvenile crime, depression, shattered relationships, and more.

What is happening? If most of the major societal problems we face can be traced back to the failure of men, why aren't men in the Church doing any better than men outside of the Church?

The answer? We are not forming men as disciples to be committed followers of Jesus Christ. Our local churches are not effective in helping men understand what it takes to be a godly husband, a godly father, and a godly man.

THE NUMBERS AREN'T PRETTY

The following excerpts from the article "Praying for Men: What Will Bring Them Back to the Church," by Henry Brinton, speak volumes as to why forming men as disciples is so important.[14]

> A 2002 survey of more than 300,000 worshipers in more than 2,000 congregations found that attendance at Catholic liturgies is 65% female, mainline Protestant attendance is 64% female, and conservative Protestant attendance is 61% female.
>
> But does this imbalance have any real effect on the Church, and beyond that the community? I'm convinced it does. An intriguing Swiss study from 1994 found that the religious practice of the father deter-

> mines the future church participation of the children. 33% of children whose parents both attended regularly will keep up the practice. However, only 2% of those whose dad is not practicing will continue to go to church even if mom is dedicated to attendance. If dad attends and mom doesn't, the percentage of children who continue to practice rises significantly. A 1997 study by Northwestern University and University of Michigan researchers found that church attendance by fathers is associated with higher levels of educational attainment for both sons and daughters.

When men are involved in church, they develop a set of relationships beyond the workplace and its competitive environment. These relationships are critical to male well-being, because they provide not only acceptance and encouragement but also accountability. They challenge men to remain faithful to their families, friends, and communities. I believe that if men are not honored for their efforts and encouraged when they struggle, they tend to shirk responsibilities and pursue personal pleasures, leaving behind broken families and communities bereft of strong role models. Society suffers if it is full of weak and wandering men. Women don't have trustworthy partners, children grow up without fathers, and the young lose a sense of what it means to be a real man.

Imagine taking eighteen men to a baseball field, breaking them up into two teams, and giving them helmets, bats, a ball, and gloves. Now imagine that only one of them had seen a baseball game. What would happen? It would be chaos! Men would be throwing balls at each other and chasing each other around the field. They would ask questions like, "Why are there three rubber squares and one rubber pentagon?" or "What's with these huge gloves? They just wouldn't get it. That's what is happening in our culture today. Not enough Catholic men are learning how to be men of God, so we suffer divorce, fatherlessness, crime, and other societal problems.

START WITH THE MEN

Reducing these ills will not come from social reforms alone. It will come from spiritual reforms. What we need is nothing less than a moral and spiritual reformation of society.

Think about this for a moment: Is there any way we can get society right if we don't first get parishes right? If that is true, then is there any way we can get parishes right if we don't first get families right? If that is true, is there any way we can get families right, if we don't first get marriages right? And if that is true, is there any way we can get marriages right if we don't first get men right?

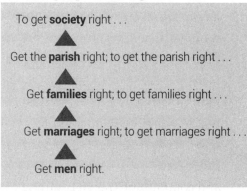

To get **society** right . . .

▲

Get the **parish** right; to get the parish right . . .

▲

Get **families** right; to get families right . . .

▲

Get **marriages** right; to get marriages right . . .

▲

Get **men** right.

How then do we get men right? We disciple them to be faithful Catholics who are deeply committed to the Lord Jesus Christ! A spiritual renewal of society starts with a spiritual renewal of men. "Everyone who follows Christ does so because the Father draws him and the Spirit moves him" (CCC, 259).

Can this be done? More importantly, will it work? It has been done before: "For God so loved the world that he gave his one and only Son," Jesus, who gathered around Himself twelve regular men, and together they changed the world.

THE MISSION: OUR MARCHING ORDERS

Matthew 28 contains the single most effective speech ever delivered. More millions of people and billions of dollars have been mobilized by this speech than any other in human history:

> "Go therefore and make disciples of all nations, baptizing them in the name of the Father and of the Son and of the Holy Spirit, teaching them to observe all that I have commanded you; and lo, I am with you always, to the close of the age." (Matthew 28:19–20)

Who would have thought this brief speech, given to a ragtag group of men, most of whom had probably never been more than forty-five miles or so from their homes, would have resulted in billions of people following Jesus Christ? Who were these guys? They were men just like the ones you have at your parish:

- Some small business owners—Peter, James, and John, who were fishermen
- A snob—Nathanael, who said "Nazareth! Can anything good come from there?"
- A religious guy—Simon the Zealot
- A government employee—Matthew, the tax collector

- Young guys in their early twenties or even younger—Andrew, and maybe all of them

Jesus discipled these men, and they changed the world. If you will disciple the men of your parish to be strong in their Catholic faith, receive the sacraments frequently, maintain an active prayer life, seek to have a closer relationship with Christ, and grow in holiness together with other men, what will happen? Marriages will improve, then families, then the parish, the Church, and finally the world.

The Church is already lacking male members. In the average church in America, there are more women than men. Think about it: Why would God give our churches more men when we are doing such an inadequate job forming disciples out of the ones we already have? And why would a man want to go to a church where many men he sees look almost identical to the ones who don't go?

We need to start with men. They need to be discipled. If they aren't, they will eventually find something else to hold their attention.

The BIG Idea

A spiritual reformation of society starts with a spiritual reformation of men.

THE STAKES: A PERSONAL STORY

It's a story we hear too often. In fact, Patrick (Pat) Morley, one of the authors of the original *No Man Left Behind*, says his father lived it. His dad was abandoned by his father at age two. He and his three siblings were raised by a single mom:

> She did a great job. But [my dad] never felt the scratch of his dad's whiskers, never smelled his work clothes, never heard him whistle while he worked, never heard him read a bedtime story, never watched how he did chores. He never saw his dad wink at his mom, never heard him say, "I love you, son," or, "I'm proud of you, son." Without a dad, he had to "guess" at what it meant to be a man, a husband, and a father.

When his dad turned six, he went to work with his older brother on a bread truck and paper route before school. They got up at three o'clock in the morning and had a permanent tardy slip to school. You see, when a man fails, he doesn't just ruin his own life. He usually takes down a good woman and two, three, or four children with him. Pat continues:

> When my dad became an adult, he had to decide if he would repeat the sins of his father or break the cycle. He really wanted to break the cycle, so when Dad had four boys of his own, our family joined a church for help. Unfortunately, our church had a vision to put my dad to work, but no vision to disciple him to be a godly man, husband, and father. As a result, my dad became successful as a worker, but as a disciple he got left behind. So, at the age of forty, when he was the top lay leader in the church (I was in the tenth grade, and my younger brothers were in the seventh, fifth, and third grades), he and my mother just got burned out, and we left the church.

> The results have been tragic. That single decision put our family into a tailspin from which, over forty years later, we have still not fully recovered: two high-school dropouts, drug addiction, alcoholism, employment problems, and divorce. One brother died of a heroin overdose. It has been more than three quarters of a century since my dad was abandoned by his father, and forty years after our family dropped out of church.
>
> I can't help but wonder how our family would have been different if our church had offered a men's discipleship ministry. I will never know. But I hope the men in your church and their sons and daughters will.

Q & A

How long did Jesus take to pick his disciples?

You might think that Jesus called each of the Twelve the first time he saw them. Luke 6 indicates that after spending quite some time in ministry with a larger group of followers, Jesus spent a *whole night in prayer*. And in the morning, "He called his disciples to him and chose twelve of them whom he also designated apostles" (verse 13). Jesus invited them into ministry with Him early but it was only after spending time—up to two years—and a whole night in prayer that He designated them as part of the inner twelve.

Obviously, he will never know, but the men in your church can. Your church can break the cycle. As Pat says:

> God brought the gospel into my family line through my wife's family line. My wife led me to Christ and, in

> turn, I was able to help introduce Dad, Mom, and two brothers to Christ as their Savior. Our two children love Christ and have both married Christian spouses.

So, by God's grace, he did break the cycle, but it took two generations instead of one.

What was the difference between Pat and his father? Pat got involved in a church that had a vision to disciple him to live like Christ—a church committed to making sure he was not left behind.

Pat's dad and mom both died in 2002. If his dad were still alive, Pat would say to him, "Dad, I know you wanted to break the cycle. I know that things didn't turn out like you dreamed. But Dad, we have broken the cycle. Sure, it took two generations instead of one. But God has done it."

Pat knows that if his dad were still alive, he would say, "I am responsible for taking us out of church." That's admirable. However, the church must also accept culpability. The church leaders had a vision for putting his dad to work, but they didn't have a vision for helping him become a disciple.

NO MORE MEN LEFT BEHIND

Pat's dad was a good man. He didn't want to fail. If he could have seen what was coming around the bend, he would have made a different decision. He never saw it coming. His church, on the other hand, should have seen it coming. It's time to fix this system so that future generations of men become disciples and don't get left behind.

You probably have a man in your parish just like Pat's dad—trying to be a good man, full of good intentions, full of hopes and dreams for his family, a man who wants to break the cycle. He is a man looking to you for guidance. His sons and daughters may be in your youth group, and they have no idea what is about to happen when Dad stops coming to church. Please, for the sake of Christ and his kingdom, identify that man and disciple him to be a godly man, husband, and father.

Pat can testify how important this is. His dad's church missed its moment. From that one error his family has suffered needlessly for over forty years. It doesn't have to happen to your men. You can build a system that God can use to disciple every man in your parish.

Wanting to do something is not the same as doing it. What kind of men are you trying to make? The next chapter will help you define a disciple so that you can know what you are trying to produce.

Remember This . . .

- Many of today's cultural problems can ultimately be traced back to the failure of a man.
- No man fails on purpose.
- Men in the Church face the same problems and issues as men outside of the Church.
- Few men are involved in any discipleship activity outside of Sunday Mass.
- Jesus poured his life and ministry into twelve young men. On these men he built the Church.

- If you disciple men, marriages will improve, then families, then parishes, the Church, and finally the world.
- Our parishes need a vision for building disciples, not just putting people to work.

Talk About This . . .

1. Are we giving men a bum rap when we say that most of the cultural problems we face can be traced to the failure of a man? Why or why not?
2. Do the women outnumber the men in your parish? What is the ratio of men to women? What are some of the reasons for this? What difference will it make?
3. All of us know men who have failed—in their marriages, careers, relationships with kids—even though they had no intention of failing. What do you think happened?
4. Estimate the percentage of men in your parish actively involved in discipleship. What are some of the opportunities for discipleship that your parish offers men? What are some of the reasons that the men who are involved got involved? What are some of the reasons that men who are not involved stayed on the outside?

Pray About This . . .

Pray together as a leadership team:

- That God will give the leadership of your parish a renewed vision for the importance of forming men as disciples.
- That God will work in the lives of specific men you know who are failing in some way—spiritually, emotionally, physically, financially, and relationally.
- That God will continue to bond your hearts together in a shared vision to disciple every man in your parish, and that he will call more leaders in your church to this vision.

3
WHAT IS A DISCIPLE?

"What exactly is a disciple?" It's a great question—you have to know what you are trying to produce before you implement a system to produce it! This chapter will discuss the motivations of men, define "disciple," and describe a process by which men become disciples of Jesus Christ.

THE *CATECHISM OF THE CATHOLIC CHURCH* describes a disciple in this way: "The disciple of Christ must not only keep the faith and live on it, but also profess it, confidently bear witness to it, and spread it" (CCC, 1816).

In our experience with men and men's leaders, we have found three things that all men want:

- *something* to give their lives to,
- *someone* to share it with, and
- a *personal system* that offers a reasonable explanation why the first two are so difficult!

This is perfectly illustrated in Ecclesiastes, when Solomon writes:

> . . . a person who has no one, either son or brother, yet there is no end to all his toil, and his eyes are never satisfied with riches, so that he never asks, "For whom am I toiling and depriving myself of pleasure?" This also is vanity and an unhappy business. (Eccelesiastes 4:8)

WHAT DO MEN WANT?

All men want something to give their lives to: a mission, a cause, or a purpose. Every man wants to get to the end of his life and feel like it counted for something, like he mattered. For many, like the man in Ecclesiastes, they find this in their work. They want to build a company, a career—or at least a bank account—that others will look at with respect and admiration. For other men it's charitable work, or the homeowners association, or their kids' accomplishments.

The common thread is this: Men want to be involved in something bigger than themselves, something that is meaningful.

In addition to something to give their lives to, men want someone to share their lives with. John Eldredge refers to this as "a beauty to win." Typically it includes marriage, but it goes beyond marriage as well. A man "with neither son nor brother" soon finds his toil is "meaningless." Contrary to popular opinion, men were made for relationships; those relationships just might not look like Oprah thinks they should. How else would we explain the popularity of fraternities, softball teams, and bars?

All of us are looking for meaning, happiness, peace, tranquility, contentment. By default, a man will look for satisfaction primarily in his accomplishments (something to give his life to) and in other people (someone to share it with). But most men will also tell you they are frustrated with the difficulty of finding success in accomplishment and relationships. Most of the "systems" that men buy into seem to answer either one problem or the other: Work as hard as you can to build a successful career, stay late, take on the big projects, travel on a moment's notice. But a system designed to maximize your career will undermine your ability to have meaningful relationships in your life. You might build a prosperous lifestyle, but you will have no one to enjoy it with.

Alternatively, you can build a life that depends on other people. Have you seen the sitcom *Cheers*? Everyone yells "Norm!" when the lovable accountant strolls into his favorite watering hole. But his dedication to the guys at the bar undermines every other relationship and responsibility in his life.

Every man has to decide what he believes will make him happy. A man who puts his faith in his career or achievements will soon find that the world constantly asks the same question: "What have you done for me lately?" Fail to perform and the party's over. A man who puts his faith in relationships with others will find that his friends—or even his wife—are his best buddies until he puts his own needs in front of theirs. It's a variation on the same theme. At some point the man will decide he needs a new job, new friends, or a new wife. Eventually he will say, "This also is vanity and an unhappy business."

WHAT DO MEN NEED?

The obvious answer to the question "What do men need?" is that they need the gospel of Jesus Christ. Faithfulness to God, placing Him foremost in their life, is the one system that really works—a system that *helps men change the core affections of their hearts*. As St. Augustine, who sought fulfillment in sensual pleasure, honor, and ambition, put it in his *Confessions*: "You have made us for yourself, and our hearts are restless until they rest in you."

In the gospel, in the encounter with Jesus Christ, there is a relationship that redefines every aspect of our life by giving it new meaning. We can call this a "system," because it reaches every corner of life, by placing Jesus Christ at the center. We can look to the Gospels to understand who Jesus is, what he has done for us, and how he refashions our life.

This process of helping men move from relying on themselves or others to relying on God is discipleship. As the model shows, it is a process of deepening a man's relationship with God. But just exactly what does it mean to be a "disciple"?

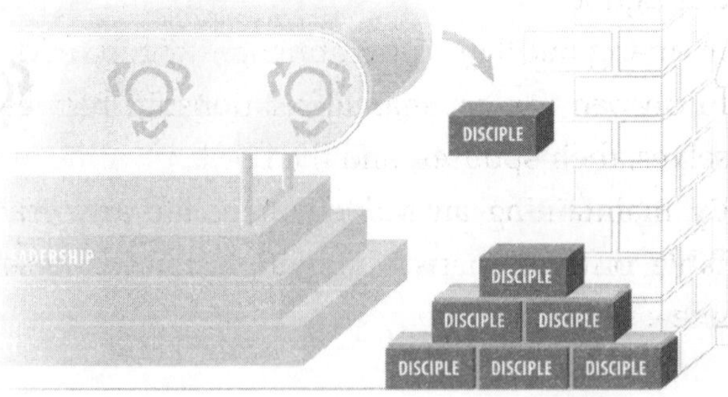

"DISCIPLE" DEFINED

In the Bible, the word for *disciple* literally means "pupil" or "learner." When applied to the early Christians, it came to mean someone who declared a personal and communal allegiance to the teachings and person of Jesus. Today, the life of a disciple revolves around Jesus.

We would like to suggest three conditions that, if met, qualify a person to be counted as a disciple. All three conditions must be present. Further, if these three conditions are met, the person should not claim to not be a disciple.

First, Catholic disciples are called to walk with Christ; they profess Christ and they live their lives in the following ways:

- By living fully into the sacraments of initiation (baptism and confirmation)
- By participating at Mass fully and faithfully—not only by being there each week but by worshiping God through the reception of the Eucharist
- By understanding that the reason we participate at Mass is to worship God with our heart, mind, and body
- By making use of the sacrament of reconciliation on a regular basis to obtain the sanctifying grace that comes through it
- By living out their commitment to their wedding vows to deepen the covenantal relationship between themselves, their spouses, and the Lord
- By maintaining an active prayer life and reading the Bible, offering thanksgiving and praise, and seeking to live a Christlike life

Second, disciples are equipped to live like Christ; they are engaged in an ongoing process of training for spiritual growth and transformation.

Third, disciples are sent to work for Christ; they are servants of the Lord, the salt of the earth, the light of the world. Disciples are God's hands and feet, sent to evangelize the whole world. "Amen, I say to you, whatever you did for one of these least brothers of mine, you did for me" (Matthew 25:40).

At the Last Supper Jesus washed the disciples' feet and commanded them to do likewise. A strong, active, committed Catholic disciple puts all his intellectual knowledge and spiritual knowledge to work for Christ by serving and helping others. A committed man serves God with his time, talents, and treasure.

First and foremost, a disciple is someone who has believed in Jesus—his life, work, death, and resurrection. The first task of making disciples is *evangelism*—to call men to a deeper walk with Christ, a deeper conversion. Pope Paul VI in his encyclical, *Evangelization in the Modern World*, said "We wish to confirm once more that the task of evangelizing all people constitutes the essential mission of the Church."[15] He went on to say:

> Evangelization will also always contain—as the foundation, center, and at the same time, summit of its dynamism—a clear proclamation that, in Jesus Christ, the Son of God made man, who died and rose from

> the dead, salvation is offered to all men, as a gift of God's grace and mercy.[16]

A lot of people who reject Catholicism see Catholics and say, "If that's what it means to be a Catholic, then I want no part of it." Isn't that a criticism too dangerous to leave unanswered? It may do more harm than good to invite a man to become a committed Catholic if we have no plan to help him truly know and follow Christ.

The second task of making disciples is *teaching*—to form them to live like Christ, i.e., to be continually transformed into the image and likeness of Christ. Forming and equipping Christians is a lifelong process. It doesn't stop. When we don't disciple a man to profess Christ with his life, he will almost always become lukewarm in faith, worldly in attitude, and hypocritical in behavior. Why do we form men to live like Christ? So they can enjoy Christ by knowing him better, but also "so that the man of God may be thoroughly equipped for every good work" (2 Timothy 3:16–17). Jesus prayed, "As the Father has sent me, I am sending you" (John 20:21).

The BIG Idea

A disciple is called to walk with Christ, equipped to live like Christ, and sent to work for Christ.

Every man wants to give his life to a cause, to make a difference, to do something with his life. When we disciple a man, he will eventually want to make that difference for the glory of God: to "bear much fruit" and do good works "that will abide" (John 15:8, 16).

The third task of making disciples is moving men toward

service—sending men forth to work for Christ, to build his kingdom, and to bring him glory. Once a man has been with Christ, experienced the joy of his grace, the warmth of his love, the cleansing of his forgiveness, and the indwelling of his Spirit, he inevitably comes to a point when he can no longer be happy unless he is serving the Lord.

HEAD, HEART, HANDS

A man is not a mature disciple until the truth is understood, believed, and lived out. Use the key words *head, heart,* and *hands* to remember these three concepts.

Head

Men must first understand the truth of the gospel. They need to grow in their knowledge of their faith.

"Always be prepared to make a defense to any one who calls you to account for the hope that is in you, yet do it with gentleness and reverence; and keep your conscience clear, so that, when you are abused, those who revile your good behavior in Christ may be put to shame." (1 Peter 3:15–16)

Sometimes, too much emphasis is placed on intellectual knowledge. Basically, every event offered by men's ministry has only a teaching focus. In this case, men with "big heads" but very small hearts and hands are produced.

Heart

Men need to have a growing conviction deep within them that the gospel is true, that God loves them as a father, and that he can be trusted. Along with knowledge, they need an emotional connection to Christ. Their worldview needs to shift so that they begin to see things from a godly perspective.

Sometimes, a men's ministry can put too much emphasis on emotion. In this case, men can come to God mainly for an emotional "fix." Instead of serving God with all of their lives, they base their Christian experience mainly on their feelings.

Hands

To really understand truth at the deepest level, you have to put it into practice. We would be unlikely to truly understand Jesus' teaching about the poor until we do something to help a poor person. We must always strive to give men the opportunity to live out what they are learning through our ministry.

Sometimes, though, we can put too much emphasis on performance or duty. In this case, men will define Christianity mainly in terms of whether they have fulfilled a certain set of rules or expectations. This easily creates workers, not disciples, and eventually alienates men from God and his grace.

In your ministry to men, strive for a balanced approach so that men learn the truth at all three levels.

Next, what are the methods you can use to actually make disciples?

HOW DO YOU MAKE A DISCIPLE?

Eucharistic Liturgy

"The sacred liturgy does not exhaust the entire activ-

> ity of the Church": it must be preceded by evangelization, faith, and conversion. It can then produce its fruits in the lives of the faithful: new life in the Spirit, involvement in the mission of the Church, and service to her unity. (CCC, 1072)

The heart of Catholic worship is the Eucharist. In it we learn who we are and who God in Jesus Christ is to us. In one of Matthew Kelly's presentations, he talks about what people say is wrong with the Mass. He lists the complaints people have, from the priest to the choir to the sound system to the air conditioning. His conclusion? *We are what's wrong with the Mass.* We are called to participate, not just show up. Christ is present Body and Blood, Soul and Divinity in the Eucharistic liturgy. He begins by welcoming us. He invites us to call to mind our failings. He offers us forgiveness. He feeds us with his Word. He offers his Body and Blood as food and drink for us. He sends us forth in peace. What more could we ask for? There is a full week of nourishment and instruction. And it is available somewhere near you every day.

Even if your schedule doesn't allow you to attend daily Mass, Jesus is present in the tabernacle of every Catholic Church.

Reconciliation

Frequent celebration of the sacrament of reconciliation, in which we confess our sins to Christ and receive his forgiveness, keeps us humble and helps us to be aware of the temptation to sin that is all around us.

Small Groups

Every major leader in ministry to men today lists small groups as key for discipleship. A man we know read *The Man in the Mirror* and accepted the challenge to start an accountability group. That group grew to eight men, then split into four groups. Two of the men approached the pastor to start a men's ministry. After seven years, about seventy-five other groups existed with an estimated nine hundred men. Small groups are a dynamic way to build disciples.

What kinds of small groups are there?

- Bible studies
- Accountability groups
- Prayer groups
- Sharing groups
- Groups for men only
- Couples' groups
- Home (cell) groups
- Office groups

Meaningful change often takes place in the context of small-group relationships. As men tell their "stories," the truth of the gospel takes on flesh and bones. Simply put, we just "get it" better when we see the gospel lived out in our lives!

Private Study

Do your men lack power? Jesus said, "You are wrong, because you know neither the scriptures nor the power of God" (Matthew 22:29). Men become disciples when they discover God in his Word. Although men can have life-changing experiences that alter the way they relate to God, it is most important that men spend time reading and studying the Bible. St. Jerome said, "Ignorance of Scripture is ignorance of Christ." Have you ever known a single man whose life has changed in any significant way apart from the regular study of God's Word? Ask a man who has a close relationship with Christ, and you will find he spends private time praying and reading God's Word every day. Along with frequent Communion, he is convinced that it helps him walk closely with Jesus.

Encourage men to use private study time or group study to memorize meaningful verses, pray, sing, and meditate on God's Word. We speak to God in prayer and God often speaks to us through the Scriptures. The National Fellowship of Catholic Men offers a great book for memorizing Scripture, *The Catholic Topical Memory System: Hiding God's Word in Your Mind and Heart*, by Rich Cleveland. This book can be used by individual Catholic men or with other men in small groups.

Spiritual Reading

We have an opportunity to go deeper into our understanding of our relationship with God and obtain closeness with him by reading the works of men and women who have achieved a level of understanding to which we can aspire. The classic books are a great place to start, with such titles as *The Imitation of Christ, The Cloud of Unknowing, The Spiritual Exercises, The Confessions, The Ascent of Mount Carmel, The Interior Castle, The Story of a Soul,* and others. There are many more recent authors that we would do well to read too, such as G. K. Chesterton, C. S. Lewis, St. John Paul II, Pope Francis, and many others. These people have been gifted with the ability to inspire us to follow Jesus. They are able to articulate a better understanding of how God works in our life. There are so many excellent opportunities to learn how to deepen our relationship with Christ and develop a deeper spirituality. God uses books to speak to a man and inspire him to make a change in life. We see over and over that a man will get hold of a book, and God will use the book to get hold of the man. Give a guy a book!

Q & A

How do some men always seem to have the right verse or passage whenever they need it?

Many men who do this have something in common. It's not a photographic memory. It's journaling. Try keeping a small notebook beside you and jotting down notes and reflections whenever you read the Bible or a Christian book. Also consider memorizing Scriptures that have made an impact on you (Psalm 119:9, 11).

Conferences and Seminars

Men often say, "Wow, that Catholic men's conference changed my life!" This is discouraging to some priests. They think, Those speakers didn't say anything to my men that I haven't been saying for years! But it's just like bringing someone in to preach a parish mission. If the local priests hadn't laid the groundwork with their homilies and teachings, the ground of the men's hearts would not have been prepared to receive the message delivered by the conference speakers.

Informal Discussions

Some of the richest times of our lives are found "hanging out" with buddies. Whether it's going to lunch, riding motorcycles, or talking theology with friends, God often orchestrates teachable moments to build into each other's lives.

Leadership Training

Pat Morley's father-in-law says, "Amateurs teach amateurs to be amateurs." We agree. If you are serious about making disciples, you should get some training. Just as discipleship requires training and lifelong learning, so does good ministry to men.

All these activities can help a man know Christ, but how will you offer them something strategically? How can you make sure activities are more than a set of hoops that a man jumps through to justify himself before God? In the next chapter, we will look at how men change and how God can use your system to change their hearts.

Remember This . . .

- Every man wants something to give his life to, someone to share it with, and a system that gives a reasonable explanation for why the first two are so difficult.
- Men often look for success in accomplishments and relationships.
- Every man needs a system that helps him change the core affections of his heart—the gospel.
- A disciple is someone who is called to walk with Christ, equipped to live like Christ, and sent to work for Christ (see 2 Timothy 3:15–17).

- We make disciples by evangelizing, teaching, and providing opportunities to serve.
- A mature disciple understands, believes, and lives out the truth of the gospel with his head, hands, and heart.
- There are many methods to make disciples which your parish is probably already using.

Talk About This . . .

1. What are some examples of ways men seek a sense of purpose and significance? In what ways—good or sinful—do men seek "someone" to share their lives with?
2. What are some of the "systems" men you know use to explain life? What difference does this make in their life?
3. How have you seen the gospel change a man's spiritual life in your parish or community? Share what happened and how it impacted you. How have you seen the gospel change your life?

Pray About This . . .

Pray together as a leadership team:

- That men in your parish and community would turn to Christ to find a sense of purpose, significance, and fulfillment.
- That God would engage men's hearts, minds, souls, and strength in drawing them closer to himself, and give them a vision for building his kingdom.

4

HOW DO MEN CHANGE? HELPING MEN EXPERIENCE SPIRITUAL TRANSFORMATION

In the previous chapters we gave you some tools to define what a disciple looks like. It would be natural for you to ask, "How does a man become one?" This chapter helps you understand how a man changes and why your ministry should focus on helping men change the core affections of their hearts. You can create a wonderful discipleship system, but if you leave men to themselves, they will simply go through the motions. Pay close attention to this chapter so your ministry won't lack the power to truly transform men's lives.

A LEADER TOLD US the story of "Lou," a man he met in a small group shortly after moving to a parish. Lou and his wife had been in that parish for more than fifteen years. He had been involved in several ministries. He had a wonderful wife; his kids were active in the parish. On the outside, everything looked great. A few months of sitting in the small group did nothing to change anyone's opinion. Lou didn't speak out a lot, but when he did, it was worth listening to.

One day, this man got a call from Lou's small-group leader. Lou had left his wife and kids. He had been having an affair for several months and was taking some time to "figure out what he wanted to do." He never came back. How can this happen? How can a man sit in a small men's group, serve in ministries in his church, seem like the great father in a great family, and then one day just chuck it all?

MEN IN AMERICA: THE STRUGGLE OF SELF-RELIANCE

In Habakkuk, God describes the Babylonian army that is threatening Jerusalem:

> Dread and terrible are they;
> Their justice and dignity proceed from themselves . . .
> Then they sweep by like the wind and go on,
> Guilty men, whose own might is their god! (Habakkuk 1:7, 11)

In other words, God is saying that the Babylonians are a law to themselves (they do whatever they want), they promote their own honor (they look out for number one), and their own strength is their God (they rely on themselves). Sounds like many men today.

This is our fundamental struggle. Every moment of every day we choose either to live out of our own strength and be independent from God, or to depend on God and walk by faith. The system of this world is almost perfectly designed to encourage our men to rely on their own strength. It is easy for our projects and pressures to become more real to us than Jesus. Instead of walking by faith, we let our strength become our god. Then we become controlling, angry, panicked, bitter, defensive, proud, and withdrawn.

Performance Versus Faith

How are men successful in the world? We quickly figure out that we have to dress a certain way, have a certain job, make a certain amount of money, live in the right house, or have a good family. The focus is on external things that we can do or see.

So we take a man from this world's system and plop him down in a parish. He wants to be a "successful Catholic." He looks around and decides he needs to dress a certain way, use certain phrases, attend Mass each week, give money, and serve on a committee. Often we take a man from one performance-oriented culture (the world) and move him right into another one (the parish).

In both of these scenarios a man is basically relying on his own strength to be his god. We end up with men who are focused on whether their external behavior matches some ideal, but who are disconnected from a heart of faith.

Men know how to play the game, and, if you let them, they will follow your rules to perfection. The only problem is that in ten or twenty years, like Lou, they will realize that their hearts are dead.

Why Is This So Important?

Would you say the following statement is true or false (go with your first reaction): "Every man does exactly what he wants to do"?

It's actually something of a trick question, since it depends on how you define the word *want*.

In what sense is this statement false? Every man has good intentions on which he doesn't follow through—that's why the price of gym memberships rises in January and drops in March. And men often conform to others' expectations rather than behave how they might otherwise. Paul himself said, "I do not understand my own actions. For I do not do what I want, but I do the very thing I hate" (Romans 7:15).

Yet there is also a profound sense in which this statement is true. At the moment of decision, a man chooses to do one thing over another. Even when facing outside pressure or temptation, he evaluates the pros and cons and chooses what he believes will bring the greatest happiness. Whether a man gives in to lust and views pornography on the Internet or sacrificially loves his wife and hangs the curtains, he makes choices based on his worldview and beliefs. Actions are the last step in a process that starts with our attitudes, faith, and desires.

Pascal said it this way: "Happiness is the motive of every action of every man, even of those who hang themselves." Jonathan Edwards said, "The will is the mind choosing."

Jesus too makes it clear that what we do comes from our hearts. He says that "out of the abundance of the heart the mouth speaks" (Matthew 12:34) and indicates that a good tree brings forth good fruit, but a bad tree brings forth bad fruit (see Matthew 12:35).

He makes this even more explicit in Matthew 15:18–20, when he says, "What comes out of the mouth proceeds from the heart, and this defiles a man. For out of the heart come evil thoughts, murder, adultery, fornication, theft, false witness, slander. These are what defile a man." The external actions of a man are motivated by his worldview and beliefs.

We must get beyond a performance orientation. A man's actions will eventually reflect what is happening in his heart. Just like you can't treat cancer by putting a Band-Aid on a man's skin, you can't help a man become a disciple by fixing his behavior and allowing him to ignore his spiritual life. *Christianity is not about behavior modification; it's about spiritual transformation. In other words being transformed ever more perfectly into the image and likeness of Christ causes a man to live out his life in Christ through his actions.*

Do men go to Mass on Sunday (behavior-habit) or enter into the Eucharist and therefore become Eucharist (spiritual conversion-renewal)? In the words of St. John Paul II, in *Ecclesia de Eucharistia*:

> Incorporation into Christ, which is brought about by Baptism, is constantly renewed and consolidated by sharing in the Eucharistic Sacrifice, especially by that full sharing which takes place in sacramental communion. We can say not only that *each of us receives Christ*, but also that *Christ receives each of us*. He enters into friendship with us: "You are my friends" (John 15:14). Indeed, it is because of him that we have life:

> "He who eats me will live because of me" (John 6:57). Eucharistic communion brings about in a sublime way the mutual "abiding" of Christ and each of his followers: "Abide in me, and I in you" (John 15:4).
>
> By its union with Christ, the People of the New Covenant, far from closing in upon itself, becomes a "sacrament" for humanity, a sign and instrument of the salvation achieved by Christ, the light of the world and the salt of the earth (cf. Matthew 5:13–16), for the redemption of all. The Church's mission stands in continuity with the mission of Christ: "As the Father has sent me, even so I send you" (John 20:21). From the perpetuation of the sacrifice of the Cross and her communion with the body and blood of Christ in the Eucharist, the Church draws the spiritual power needed to carry out her mission. The Eucharist thus appears as both *the source* and *the summit* of all evangelization, since its goal is the communion of mankind with Christ and in him with the Father and the Holy Spirit.[17]

Friendship with the Lord

To achieve this, it is not enough to follow Jesus and to listen to him outwardly; it is also necessary to live with him and like him. This is only possible in the context of a relationship of deep familiarity, imbued with the warmth of total trust. This is what happens between friends. That's why Jesus said one day:

> Greater love has no man than this, that a man lay down his life for his friends. . . . No longer do I call

> you servants, for the servant does not know what his master is doing; but I have called you friends, for all that I have heard from my Father I have made known to you. (John 15:13, 15)

You have no doubt known men like Lou. They learn to look like a man who is walking with Christ, but their hearts are not being transformed from the inside out. After years of conforming to other people's expectations, a temptation or crisis comes along, and they decide to do what they really want to do. Like Bill Murray's character in the movie *Groundhog Day*, they finally say, "I'm not going to live by their rules anymore." And so what was buried in their hearts is revealed when they walk away from Christ.

The BIG Idea

Christianity is not about behavior modification; it's about spiritual transformation.

CREATING AN ENVIRONMENT GOD CAN USE TO CHANGE MEN'S SPIRITUAL LIVES

How can you keep what happened to Lou from happening to your men? Many parishes rely heavily on information to help men become disciples. Men need to know the truth, but intellectual knowledge is not enough to change a heart. For instance, every person who smokes in America knows smoking causes cancer, yet most continue to smoke.

What kinds of things does God typically use to touch a man's heart? Consider your own life. What is one of the most moving experiences you've had in the last few months? When was the last time you cried for a reason other than grief? What has God used to move you forward in your relationship with Him?

When we ask these questions about what moves us, here are some of the answers that men's leaders have given us:

- ***Prayer.*** God often uses times of prayer—especially being prayed for—to touch a man's heart. Talking to God and listening for his voice cause men to become open to being transformed by the Holy Spirit. Help men enter into times of personal prayer and prayer with one another. Easily the richest times are when men share their needs and pray for one another.
- ***Music.*** Once at a men's event, a young woman sang a song about a father. It included a verse that told of a young girl who got out of bed late at night and saw her father looking at pornography on a computer. When she was finished singing, there wasn't a dry eye in the room. God used that song in a way that was different from anything else accomplished through the rest of the seminar.
- ***Drama/film clips***. All of us have been moved by particularly poignant scenes from movies or plays. Use high-quality drama to help men get out of their normal way of thinking.
- ***Testimonies and stories.*** Men connect with stories. You probably know a man in your parish whose story has been a tremendous encouragement to you. Help men learn to share their experiences and give them a venue to hear what God is doing in the lives of others.
- ***Activities.*** If you're like most men, you vividly remember a conversation you had with a man while fishing or

throwing the football. God wired men for movement, tasks, and activities. Get men moving so God can touch their hearts.

- ***Shared experiences.*** God uses trials, challenges, and adventure to bond men to one another. Does your ministry get men into situations where they can relate and rely on one another? Competition, service projects, mission trips, or working together on a ministry team for the parish can all help men reach a new level of brotherhood.
- ***Relationships.*** Most of what it means to be a disciple is caught, not taught. Men's spiritual lives change as they "do life" together with other men. Consider your own life; much of what you know about being a man was probably learned from other men who invested in your life.
- ***Children.*** Men get emotional about their kids. Find ways to connect them with their children and other children who need help. Early in his marriage, a men's ministry leader joined a parenting class at his church that began with a family outing. Without telling the class members what he was doing, the teacher took pictures of all the children at the event. The next Sunday, the teacher began the class with a slide show of the children to the song "Cat's in the Cradle." This man still remembers the moment more than twenty years later.
- ***Service to others.*** Men find a deep and lasting joy when they get out of their comfort zones and serve other people. And a disciple is sent to work for Christ. Find ways to get as many men as possible into some kind of meaningful service to people who need to see the love of Christ in action.

- ***A man committed to him.*** Many men have no real friends. Yet all men need someone who truly wants the best for them. God often uses relationships to transform a man's spiritual life.
- ***Witnessing a sacrament.*** The sacrament of matrimony, the baptism of his children, his child's first Holy Communion, the confirmation of his young adult, the forgiveness he feels in reconciliation after receiving absolution, the ordination of a priest or deacon, and the comfort he receives in the sacrament of the sick for himself or an ill and suffering loved one—these are all experiences that greatly impact a man.

Are you building these kinds of things into your men's discipleship system? Make a concerted effort to do more than just make sure men are in the right classes or groups—create an environment where God can work to change their spiritual lives.

TRUE OBEDIENCE FLOWS FROM A HEART OF FAITH

So how do you motivate a man to do the things God wants him to do? Not by just telling him what to do, but rather by helping him to want to do what God wants him to do.

> Manipulation and legalistic rule-making can make a man conform on the outside for a while—even decades. But the secret to lasting obedience is a renewed heart. Our goal is to help men believe the right things so they will live the right way.

There is really only one reason men don't build their life around their faith—they don't believe they can truly trust Christ. The Bible calls this unbelief. And since everything we do reflects what is in our hearts, all sinful attitudes and actions are a result of unbelief.

When a man works seventy hours a week just so he can get more power and money, he does so because he believes that is how he will find something that he cannot get any other way. When a man gets emotionally involved with a woman who is not his wife, he believes he will gain something that his wife, or God, cannot provide.

On the other hand, when men resist temptation and choose to do what is good, they are often motivated by faith. "By faith [Moses] left Egypt, not being afraid of the anger of the king" (Hebrews 11:27). Moses obeyed God rather than man not just because he decided he would or because someone else told him to but because he believed God.

When you work with a man, consider these questions: "How can I help his faith in God to grow?" "How can I help him understand even more fully that his hope is fulfilled only in God?" "How can I help him develop a deeper love for Jesus Christ?" A spiritual life filled with faith, hope, and love leads to an upright, obedient life.

The Fruit and the Root

During a vacation a few years ago, David Delk, one of the authors of the original book, got angry with a member of his extended family. On the surface, the issue seemed to be a disagreement over a decision regarding the kids. After he thought and prayed about what was going on in his spiritual life, he realized his anger came because someone implied he had made a mistake.

Like many men, one of the idols he often loves more than Christ is the idea of his own competence—that he is capable of accomplishing anything he attempts. So when his family member disagreed with his decision, it felt like he was being accused of being wrong regarding the children. Since he couldn't accept that he was wrong without crushing his idol, he reacted with anger to protect his illusion of competence.

Men are often encouraged to deal with anger by taking a deep breath, counting to ten, and many other techniques. But this only deals with the surface. The deeper question is, "How can we help men deal with the anger in their spiritual lives?"

Another example: Too much of the advice that has been available for men struggling with pornography has been purely behavioral. Get an Internet filter, find an accountability partner, drive home a different way so you don't pass the adult video store—all good things to do, and necessary if you struggle with this issue. But just as important is that we ask a man, "Why do you love looking at pictures of naked women more than you love Jesus? What do you think you're going to get from looking at pornography that you can't get from Christ?"

As men, we are tempted to try to fix things in our own strength by focusing on externals. So we get into an accountability group, use a budgeting system, avoid places of temptation, and add items to our calendars and to-do lists. None of these is bad, but each needs to be secondary. Often the externals deal with the fruit and not the root.

When we're confronting the issues men struggle with—anger, sexual addiction, materialism, workaholism, emotional disconnection from their wife—God calls us to move past behavior to the spiritual issues involved.

Picking Off Oranges, Taping On Apples

There are lots of orange trees in central Florida. If a person decided they didn't want an orange tree anymore, they could go out and pick every orange. Next they could go to the store, buy a bagful of apples, then come home and duct tape apples all over the tree.

But what would happen? In a few weeks, the apples would rot. Next year, the oranges would be back. The only way to get rid of the oranges for good is to dig the tree up by the roots.

Often our systems teach men to "pick oranges and tape on apples." They deal with the symptoms of sin they can see, but they don't get to the root of how their sin flows out of unbelief. So even if they are able to use willpower to control their sin for a while, eventually it comes back stronger than ever. And in the meantime, their spiritual lives are growing cold.

Christ offers men the chance to change from the roots, from the inside out. He calls us to stop making our strength our god, and start walking with Him by faith. Consider Jeremiah's words:

> Cursed is the man who trusts in man
> and makes flesh his arm,

> whose heart turns away from the LORD.
> He is like a shrub in the desert,
> and shall not see any good come.
> He shall dwell in the parched places of the wilderness,
> in an uninhabited salt land.
> Blessed is the man who trusts in the LORD,
> whose trust is in the LORD.
> He is like a tree planted by water,
> that sends out its roots by the stream,
> and does not fear when heat comes,
> for its leaves remain green,
> and is not anxious in the year of drought,
> for it does not cease to bear fruit. (Jeremiah 17:5–8)

When you help men develop their roots, you'll find more and more men moving beyond being involved in your ministry for what they can get. You'll have men who want to help other men experience what God has done for them.

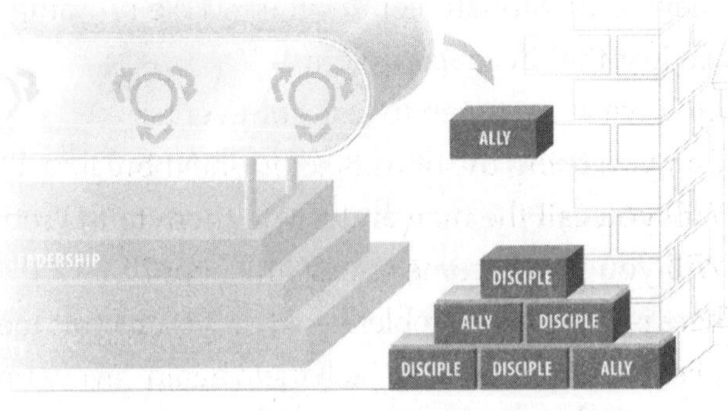

HELPING MEN BECOME ALLIES

Many men in your parish probably look at your church's ministry as a set of mostly unrelated activities and tasks (see the portal priority chart in the next chapter). And you probably spend most of your time recruiting—i.e., begging—the men who are already sitting in your church to attend your events or activities. For the first event you make an announcement, the next time you add a testimony . . . and maybe the next time you have a few skydivers land on the church lawn as Mass ends! So you spend all your time, money, creativity, and energy to get the men who are already attending Mass every week interested in your ministry to men and not much happens. And you do it over and over again, event after event, year after year. What's wrong with this picture? These are your committed men. Many of them should already feel a part of the vision and be excited about what God is doing.

How can you make a change? Men do what they want to do, and they will want to do things they see as valuable, worthwhile, or capable of bringing happiness. It's your job to present the vision in such a way that the Holy Spirit can call men to passionate commitment. (We're going to help you do just that in chapter eight.)

Often we recruit men to tasks or events:

"Can you bring the donuts to our next breakfast?"

"Will you call the men and invite them to the retreat?"

"Will you please come to our luncheon?"

There is one major problem—when you recruit men to accomplish tasks, you have to "sell them again" every time there is a new task that needs to be done or a new event to attend.

Instead, communicate about everything you do in terms

of the vision of your ministry. (Chapter eight will present a detailed discussion to help you define and communicate your vision.) If you ask a man to pick up bags of ice for the barbecue, say, "Tom, we're trying to reach every man in our parish community for Christ and help him join our band of brothers. That's why we're having this barbecue. Would you consider bringing the ice to help us reach these men and become a band of brothers?" It only takes thirty more seconds to cast the vision, and you still get your ice.

The vision will go in one ear and out the other for nineteen out of twenty men. But the payoff is with that one man. When a man buys into the vision and becomes an ally, you don't have to "sell" him on each separate activity or ministry. Each "task" becomes an opportunity for him to forward a cause he already believes in and be a disciple "sent to work for Christ."

An ally is a man who aligns himself with the vision God has given for the men of your parish. He is willing to sacrifice and work to see that vision become a reality. He may or may not formally serve on the leadership team, but he is convinced that discipling men is a cause worth giving his life to. You don't have to beg an ally to be involved—he's grateful for opportunities to advance his ministry in the lives of other men.

There are three spheres of ministry to men in your parish (see Figure 1). Many men's ministry leaders focus only on the total number of men involved in their ministry. For example: "Forty went on the retreat, twenty-seven came to breakfast, and nineteen are involved in small groups." These are great things to know, but you also need to focus on how many men are allies in the vision. Increase the number of allies every year and you will almost certainly have a vibrant and sustainable ministry to men. If this inner circle stops growing, watch out!

FIGURE 1

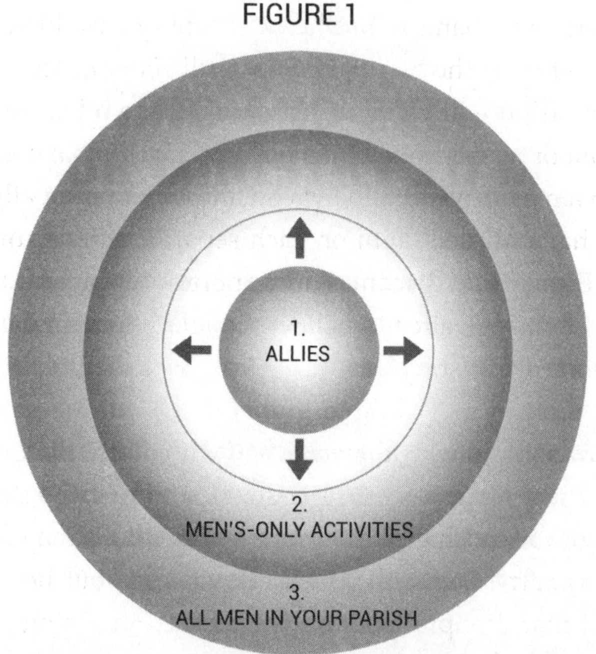

Three Spheres of Ministry to Men in Your Parish

1. The number of the men who are allies with your vision and what God is doing
2. The number of men involved in your men's-only activities—retreats, small groups, ministry projects, etc.
3. All the men who have any contact with your parish

This is why it is so important for a leadership team not to be filled with workers but rather to be praying, strategizing, recruiting, and sharing the vision with other men. Leaders burn out, their life situations change, and they move on. The way you can keep sustaining the ministry is by continuously building more and more allies within your parish.

As we've already said, men are looking to give their lives to something. Witness their commitment to golf, hunting, college football, their hobbies, and computer games. We need to lift up Christ's call in a compelling way. God will use our efforts to draw men to himself.

Create an environment in which the Holy Spirit can show men the attitudes and beliefs of their hearts. Don't allow men to go along to get along but call them into an authentic spiritual relationship with Christ. God will use your ministry not only to produce disciples but allies in the great adventure of seeing his kingdom become a reality in this world.

As God raises up allies for your ministry, be sure you know what you are actually going to do to disciple men. In the next chapter, we'll help you understand what it looks like to orient your parish around the priority of discipleship.

Remember This . . .

- Every day we choose whether to live by our own strength and be independent from God, or to depend on God and walk by faith.
- Men know how to play the game. If you let them, they will follow your rules to perfection. But in ten or twenty years, they will realize their spiritual lives are dead.

- With every decision, a man is choosing one thing over another. He makes his choices based on his worldview and his beliefs.
- Legalistic rule-making can only make a man conform on the outside for a while. The secret to lasting obedience is a renewed heart. Christ offers men the chance to change from the roots, from the inside out.
- Use methods that touch men's hearts—prayer, music, drama, film clips, testimonies, stories, relationships, and shared experiences.
- An ally is a man who aligns himself with the vision God has given for the men of your parish. He is willing to sacrifice and work to see that vision become a reality.
- One key to sustainability is to make sure you are increasing the number of allies.

Talk About This . . .

1. Why would a man seem OK on the outside, then one day just walk away from his family or his faith? Most of us have known a man who has done this. What were the circumstances?
2. Think back to a major change in your own life—quitting smoking, losing weight, etc. What caused you to make the decision to change? How would this relate to a man making a decision to allow God to change his heart?
3. Think back to a time when you had a moving experience with Christ (retreat, men's conference, etc.). What was it like? What lasting change did it bring in your life?

Pray About This . . .

Pray together as a leadership team:

- For any men in your church who are like "Lou," that they would stop going through the motions and start pursuing an authentic relationship with Christ.
- That God would help you as leaders live out an authentic and vibrant faith in Jesus Christ.
- That God would help you create an environment that he can use to touch men's spiritual lives.

PART TWO

THE FOUNDATIONS OF YOUR MINISTRY TO MEN

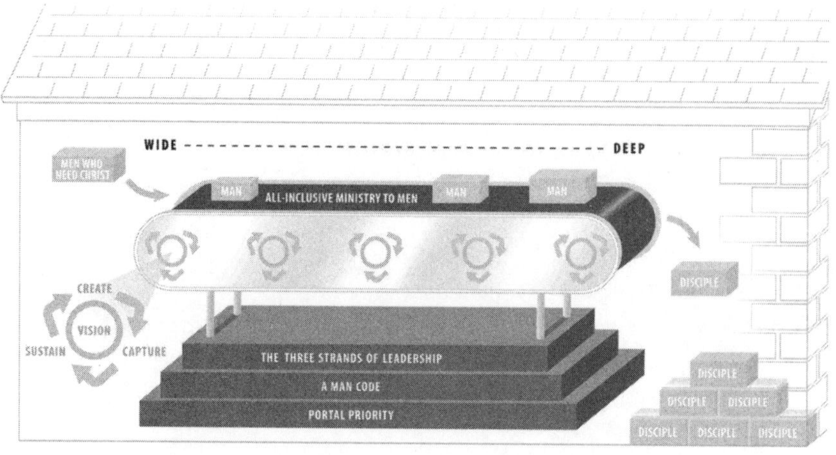

5

THE PORTAL PRIORITY AND THE MAN CODE

To build a sustainable ministry to men, you'll need a solid foundation. Start with your focus. Yes, men need to be godly fathers, caring husbands, good stewards, and servant leaders. But what is the core issue? And how can we communicate it to men so they feel valued and inspired? Laying the right foundation can help disengaged men to connect with the ministry of your parish.

SCRIPTURE TELLS US, "Go therefore and make disciples of all nations, baptizing them in the name of the Father, and of the Son, and of the Holy Spirit" (Matthew 28:19). Sometimes we get this confused with, "Go and make workers . . . browbeating them in the name of the Father and of the Son and of the Holy Spirit."

Jesus doesn't call parishes to make "workers" but "disciples." The purpose of ministry to men, then, is to make disciples, not workers. Men don't enjoy being made to go on a forced march. True disciples become workers out of the overflow of their growing relationship with Jesus Christ. Their spiritual lives are on fire for loving God, loving their fellow man, and putting into action that which they do because of the love for God.

The Bible does, however, call us to "pray" for workers: "Then he said to his disciples, 'The harvest is plentiful but the laborers are few; pray therefore the Lord of the harvest to send out laborers for his harvest'" (Matthew 9:37–38).

Too often we try to "make workers and pray for disciples." We set the agenda for our ministry and then pester men until they get involved. We make sure that we have all our slots for workers filled and then pray that somehow, some way, someone might become a disciple, a strong active committed Catholic man.

> From the beginning, Jesus associated his disciples with his own life, revealed the mystery of the Kingdom to them, and gave them a share in his mission, joy, and sufferings. Jesus spoke of a still more intimate communion between him and those who would follow him: "Abide in me, and I in you. . . . I am the vine, you are the branches" (John 21:6). And he proclaimed a mysterious and real communion between his own body and ours: "He who eats my flesh and drinks my blood abides in me, and I in him." (*CCC*, 787)

This only happens when men are continually called, equipped, and sent in the grace God gives us through the sacraments.

Here's a key idea: If your parish and men's ministry focuses on getting men to do work rather than on making disciples, it will burn them out. You will lose all your steam.

Instead, focus on making disciples and then pray that God would raise up workers for His kingdom.

A PARABLE

Picture yourself as the president of a one-hundred-person law firm. For years you have recruited lawyers but then left them on their own. Without guidance and training, they have done more harm than good. Unresolved cases have piled up, other law firms consider your firm an embarrassment, and the public thinks you are incompetent.

Suppose you go to your board of directors and ask to hire another twenty lawyers. They would say, "Are you nuts? You haven't trained the lawyers we have. Why would we let you hire more? We have a terrible reputation. In fact, several young people who interned with us have quit practicing law. You're fired!"

A law firm that doesn't produce capable lawyers is not much of a law firm at all. So what does this mean for a parish that doesn't produce disciples?

DISCIPLESHIP AS THE "PORTAL" PRIORITY

Jesus said, "Go and make disciples." That's interesting, because he could have said anything. He didn't say, "Go and make worshipers." He didn't say, "Go and make workers." Nor did He say, "Go and make good stewards." Is Jesus interested in worshipers, workers, and stewards? Of course! But he knew we wouldn't get worshipers by making worshipers, and so forth. We get worshipers, workers, and good stewards by making disciples. If a man lives this verse, "You shall love the Lord your God with all your heart, and with all your soul, and with all your strength, and with all your mind; and your neighbor as yourself" (Luke 10:27), he is a disciple.

Suppose a new family has attended your parish for three months. What will they think is the first priority—the organizing idea—of your parish? One week they heard a homily about the priority of worship. The next week they heard that they need to be good stewards of God's gifts. The following week they heard that strong committed Catholics go on mission trips. The week after that they were asked during Mass to participate in the social ministry program and attend evangelism training. The next week in the small group they joined, they learned about compelling needs at the crisis pregnancy center. A weekend seminar greatly emphasized the importance of private study and devotions. If you were a new family, what would you think? It might look like an undifferentiated blob of disjointed activities, as in Figure 2.

Looking at this collection of concepts, it is helpful to organize them into two sets: methods and outcomes. The middle items—godly families, service/missions, worship, fellowship, discipleship, evangelism, stewardship, social justice, and vocation—represent the outcomes most parishes are trying to achieve. Your parish may have more or fewer items in the list, but this is a good sampling of what most

	Preaching	Teaching	Catholic Literature	
Leadership Training	Godly Families	Service/ Missions	Worship	Bible Studies
	Fellowship	Discipleship	Evangelism	
Informal Discussions	Stewardship	Social Justice	Vocation	Private Study
	Seminars	Mentoring	Small Groups	

FIGURE 2

Undifferentiated Church Priorities and Activities
(as They Appear to a New Parishioner)

parishes want their members to understand and live out.

And yet, these are too many areas to focus on. There must be an organizing principle to help people understand, believe, and live out these objectives. That principle is discipleship.

> Discipleship is the *portal priority* through which all the other priorities of a parish can be achieved. Only by moving through the discipleship gateway can people truly affect their parish and their parish can affect them.

For instance, how can a man worship a God he doesn't know? Why would a man want to share his faith if he didn't understand the Great Commission? How could a man be a good steward if he didn't understand and believe that everything he has is a gift from God—his time, talent, and his treasures? As we disciple men's spiritual lives, they start to live out of the overflow of their relationship with Christ. Therefore, we can organize these efforts by putting discipleship in the center and drawing arrows out to each of our other priorities like this:

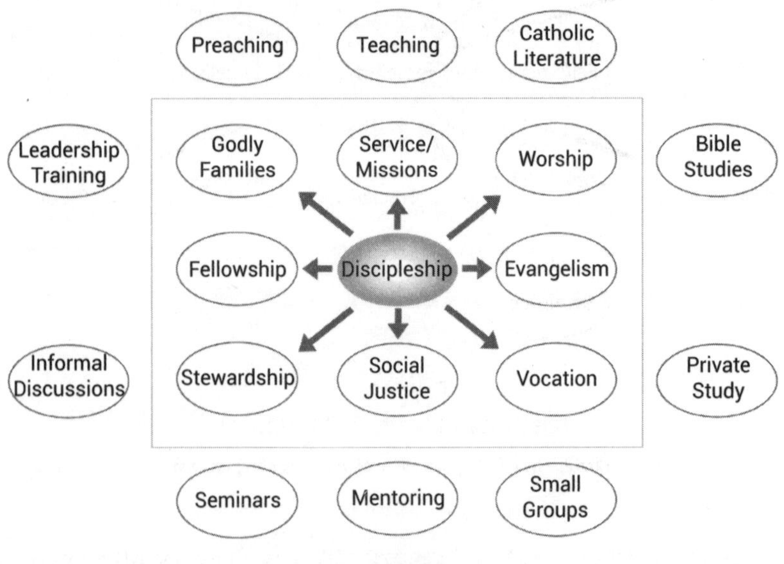

FIGURE 3

Desired Parish Outcomes
Organized Around Discipleship as the Portal Priority

How can a parish implement discipleship as the portal priority? The items around the outside of Figure 4 represent the activities, or methods, a parish engages in to help build strong, active, committed Catholic disciples.

Remember these activities are not ends in themselves but rather focus on helping people learn or live out what it means to be a strong, active, committed Catholic disciple. Figure 4 illustrates this: All activities on the outside lead to discipleship in the middle. Now we have a clear picture of

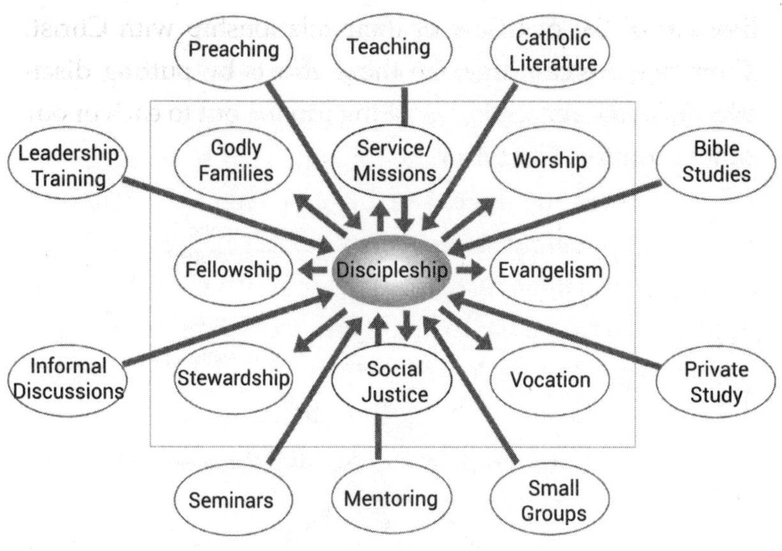

FIGURE 4

Methods of Making Disciples to Reach Other Parish Priorities and Goals

discipleship as the portal priority by which every other goal of the parish can be accomplished. For example, we don't preach to make worshipers but rather preach to help a man see God so that he can't help but worship.

To look at it a different way, rearrange *methods* and *outcomes* into two lists, with the methods of discipleship on the left, and the outcomes of discipleship on the right.

STEWARDS VERSUS DONORS

What steps might a parish take to financially support its growing ministries? First, the pastor could preach about the responsibility of parishioners to be good stewards of their time, talent and treasure. The parish council or stewardship committee could make presentation explaining the finances of the parish and might recommend books that parish ministry leaders could give all the small groups. Announcements could be placed in the bulletin with some Scripture references here and there. The finance committee could host a financial planning seminar for the parish. But if you are preaching, teaching, reading, and announcing just to get the people attending the parish to give money, you have a performance orientation. Your chart would look like Figure 5.

What's missing here is discipleship. You're not creating *stewards*; you're creating *donors*. So what does it mean to disciple men to be good stewards?

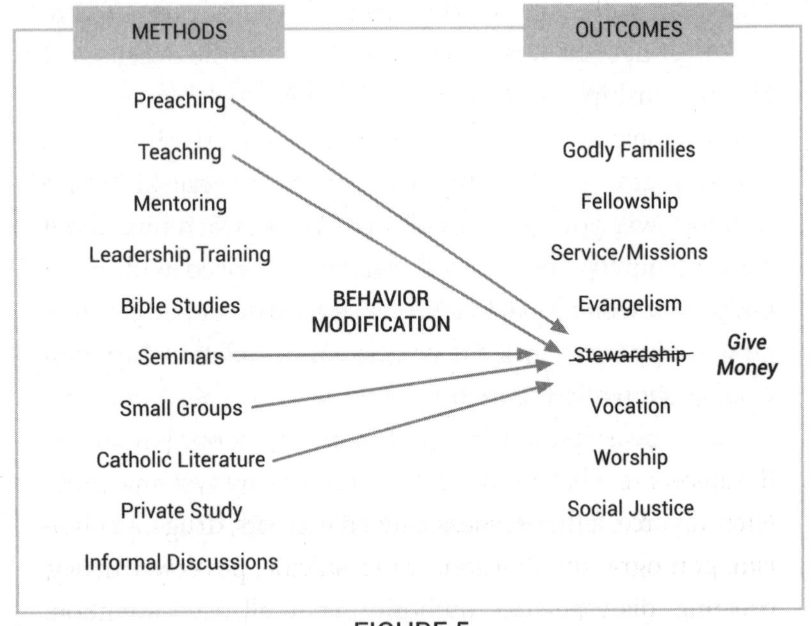

FIGURE 5

First, we would preach, teach, and so forth not to guilt or obligate men to give so that we can meet the budget. In Mark 12:30–31, Jesus answers the question, "What is the most important commandment?" by saying, "'Love the Lord your God with all your heart, and with all your soul, and with all your mind, and with all your strength.' The second is this: 'Love your neighbor as yourself.' There is no commandment greater than these."

In chapter three, we described a strong active committed Catholic disciple as "called, equipped, and sent." A man who has answered the call to give his life to Christ and is equipped as a strong active committed Catholic disciple to know God will be motivated to love God and his neighbor. That man will respond to a need when it is presented to him, not out of guilt or obligation, but out of the overflow of his relationship with Christ.

If you help a man love God with all his heart, mind, soul, and strength, and love his neighbor, then what kind of a response will you get from him when you teach him about stewardship? When you tell him about a need within the body? You won't have to tell him what to do or badger him; he will respond out of the *overflow* of his relationship with God, as shown in Figure 6.

Making discipleship the portal priority of our parishes is the answer to what ails us. Consider our many systemic problems: divorce, fatherlessness, unwed mothers, drugs, alcoholism, pornography, abortion, crime, suicide, poverty, truancy, cheating, disrespect for authority. They all need attention. Beneath everything, though, is the need for a discipleship renewal in the Catholic Church. What single activity would have the greatest impact on all of these problems twenty years from now? The formation of men as disciples today.

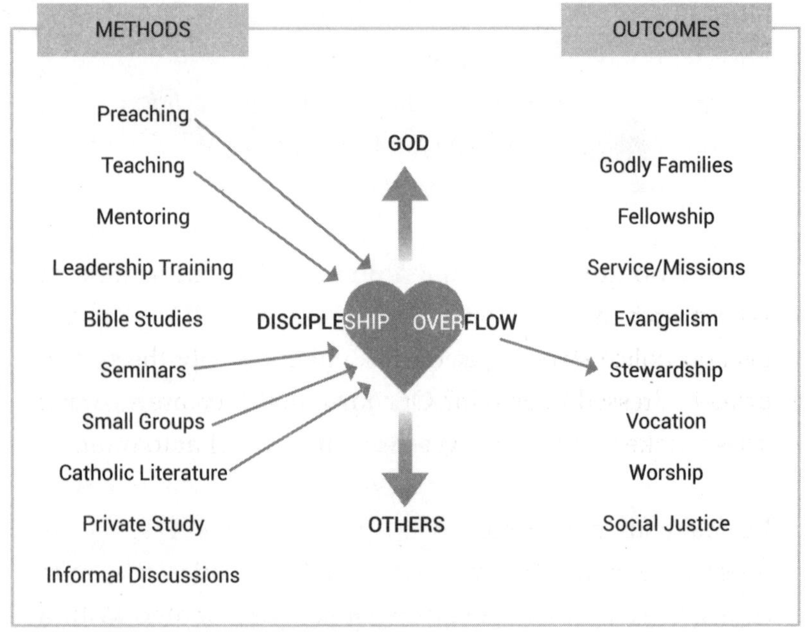

FIGURE 6
Serving God and Others
Out of an Overflowing Heart

A MAN CODE

When you make forming men as disciples your portal priority, men will notice. As a matter of fact, they are already noticing a lot more about your parish than you may think.

Quick . . . in a phrase or sentence, what's the dress code in your parish? With just a second or two of thought, you probably came up with a description of what people wear: business casual; suit and tie; cowboy boots and blue jeans.

One group from Hawaii said "shorts and thongs." (They meant sandals, of course.)

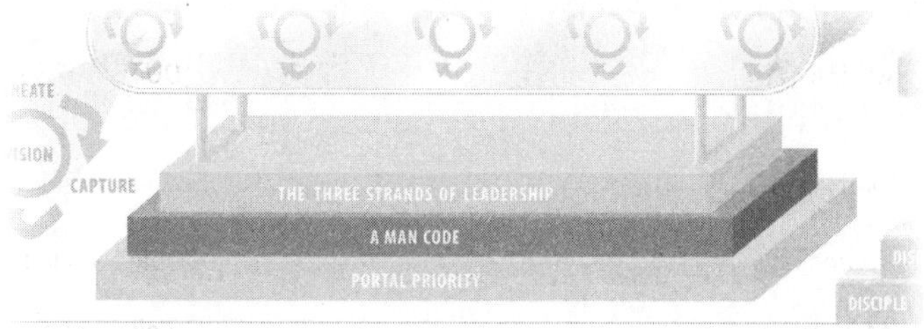

How do guys know this? Is there a sign out in front of your church that says "Shirt and Tie Required"? Do you have fashion police standing at the doors letting only the appropriately dressed people in? Of course not! Men are smart. It doesn't take more than a week to figure out what to wear.

Just as your parish has an unspoken—but well-known—dress code, it also has an unspoken "man code." The man code is the environment your parish creates for men. Within a few weeks after coming to the parish for the first time, a man understands what it means to be a man in this parish. Just like with the dress code, this impression isn't explicitly stated. Men soak it in from the atmosphere around them.

MESSAGES YOUR PARISH SENDS TO MEN

What impression does your parish give about the importance of men? How would you complete this statement: "Men are _____ here"?

"Important"? "Tolerated"? "Needed"? "Leaders"? "Supposed to do the hard work but leave the thinking to the women"?

These are some of the answers we've received from church leaders who have attended courses at the Leadership Training. One man said their man code was, "If you'd like your wife and children to go to church, bring them here." Another said, "Successful men wanted here." Another's was, "If you think you're tired now, come to our church, and we'll show you what tired really is!" Finally, one man said their man code was simply "Hi." Obviously, we've also had many positive man code statements as well.

What about your parish? Imagine a new man comes to Mass three or four times. In a phrase or sentence, how would he honestly sum up what he thinks it means to be a man in your parish? Consider this question carefully then write your man code in the space provided.

____

____

____

Since it's not something that is explicitly stated, how exactly do men figure out the "man code" of your parish?

Entire books have been written on this subject, including *Why Men Hate Going to Church,* by David Murrow (Thomas Nelson, 2005). The author points out that every church has a "thermostat." Unfortunately, many churches' thermostats are set to "comfort." Men, Murrow says, need a thermostat set to "challenge." The job

The BIG Idea

Within a few weeks, a man understands what it means to be a man in your parish.

of the pastor is to comfort the afflicted and afflict the comfortable. Men need to be "afflicted" out of their comfort zone.

Here are some other ways men learn to recognize the man code from the environment their parish creates.

Impressions from the Leaders

Men look at the leaders. Men follow strong leaders. They like to know that their leaders are certain of where they are going and what they are saying. This isn't about browbeating or blind obedience, it's about confidence. If a man doesn't believe in the leaders, he can't follow the vision.

This is particularly important to men who are either young or new to your parish. When you hold up a leader as a standard for a mature Christian man, does he look boring, tired, and half dead? Or does he look vibrant, excited, and well-spoken (regardless of age)? Men should be able to look at the visible leaders in the parish and say, "I want to be like that."

Impressions from the Music

Men listen to the music. While contemporary music may connect stylistically with the up-and-coming generations, some of those praise choruses aren't exactly "man friendly." Men resonate with songs that talk about the challenge, adventure, and battle of following Christ and seeing his kingdom become a reality. They tend to connect less with songs that ask Jesus to "hold me in your arms."

Impressions from the Bulletin

Men read the bulletin. If your parish bulletin has a section for women's ministry events, does it have a section with information for men? If not, what message does that send? More important than the amount of space the bulletin devotes to men, how does it communicate with the people in general? If your bulletin has articles in it, think about adding an article for men once in a while.

Be sure the bulletin makes strong statements about what God is doing through men in your parish. "Men's Bible Study, Wednesday night, Room 202, 7:30 P.M." is not appealing to most men. How about "Disruptive Jesus: A Bible Study for Men. Come learn how Jesus challenged the norm, and how it can have a radical impact on your life and our community. Join us on Wednesday night at 7:30 P.M. in Room 202"? Now, that's a Bible study that has a chance to catch men's attention.

Impressions from the Priest

They listen to the priest. Priests, of course, have a tremendous impact on how men are viewed in the parish. Does the priest make a point of speaking directly to men in just about every homily? Will he say, "Men, this is what this means for us . . ." That sends a clear message that men matter in his parish.

Impressions from the Setting

They look at the decor. Really . . . men notice the setting and pick up on its message. Mauve window treatments, flowery wallpaper, pastel colors—all of these can send the message to men: "We've designed this space to make our women as comfortable as possible."

Get some guys on the decorating committee! You should fight nicely to make the physical environment of your church man friendly.

Q & A

Does "man friendly" mean anti-woman?

Most women we've met would do whatever it took to get their husbands or sons into church. Women will buy this concept of making the church "man friendly" when they're shown that it will get them what they want—the men in their lives growing in their faith.

Impressions from the Level of Quality

They look for quality. Men are extremely sensitive on this issue. While there certainly need to be times when the children's choir sings in thirteen-part disharmony, the church choir should not. Men don't think it's sweet when members of the drama troupe "tried really hard" but forgot their lines. Quality extends to the flyers you hand out to men, the events you hold for them, the materials you use in small group, and even the parish website.

Men today have become savvy consumers, and they are surrounded by sophisticated, high-quality marketing all the time. While you can't expect to compete with Madison Avenue, men can tell when there is a sincere effort to offer quality. If you think about it, the message we are delivering deserves our best efforts.

Impressions from the Use of Humor

They listen for humor. For a men's ministry event, one church invited men by calling it a "mandatory meeting for all men in the parish (unless you have a problem with authority, in which case, you're not allowed to come!)." When men see that everything doesn't have to be "prim and proper" (translation: boring), they get a sense that your parish is a place where they can fit in.

At one Leadership Training class, a pastor responded to the banter between the faculty members—which is often playful and joking. He exclaimed, "I never realized that Christianity could be fun!"

A note of caution, though: Humor at the expense of men sends the wrong message. Don't make men—or an individual man—look stupid for a laugh, especially in mixed company. You would never tell racist or sexist jokes, so be careful about "stupid men" jokes.

Impressions from the Church's Vision

They listen for the vision. Men want to believe that God is doing something through your parish. They want to be part of a parish that is going somewhere. They want to know that being a man in your parish matters. Reinforce the vision of your men as often as you can in ways that will resonate with them.

THE FOUNDATIONS FOR YOUR MINISTRY

You've started building a strong foundation for your men's ministry. A philosophy of ministry that says discipleship is your portal priority puts first things first, and encourages you to always focus on forming men as disciples instead of correcting their behavior. Making sure your man code makes men feel welcome increases the likelihood they'll hang around long enough for your ministry to make an impact in their lives.

In the next chapter we'll explain how leadership forms the final layer of your foundation.

Remember This . . .

- Jesus said, "Go and make disciples." He could have picked anything—for example, workers, worshipers, or tithers. But he picked disciples.
- Discipleship is the portal through which we can achieve all the priorities of the parish.
- When discipleship is not the portal priority, we often end up focusing on men's behavior rather than their spiritual lives.
- When we disciple men to love God and their neighbors, they will live in a way that reflects this love.
- Every parish has an unspoken—but well-known—man code, an impression it gives about what it means to be a man in this parish.
- There are many cues that men pick up on to develop this impression: the leaders, music, bulletin, priest, decor, quality, and vision. Well-placed humor helps too.

Talk About This . . .

1. Do the eight outcomes shown in Figure 3 correspond with your parish's priorities? What would you add or delete?
2. How does your parish build strong, active, committed, Catholic disciples? Do you employ all of the methods on the outside of the box in Figure 4? What would you add or delete?

3. Pick an activity you are doing for men now. Does this activity focus on men's spiritual lives or their behavior? How would you adjust it to focus more on discipleship?
4. Do you think your parish has an environment that is male friendly? What does your parish do that might make men, especially new men, feel uncomfortable?
5. How could you improve your environment without making the women feel uncomfortable? Brainstorm your ideas using the list provided near the end of this chapter.

Pray About This . . .

Pray together as a leadership team:

- That God helps you focus your ministry efforts to disciple men into a right relationship with him.
- That your parish's men—and your leadership team—would live out of the overflow of their relationship with him.
- That God would help you provide a welcoming and engaging environment for men.
- That God will continue to help your leadership team grow closer as a band of brothers, devoted to forming men as disciples from the inside out.

6
THE THREE STRANDS OF LEADERSHIP

Bill Bright, founder of Campus Crusade for Christ, was fond of saying, "Everything boils down to leadership." We believe him. Our experiences with parishes that are forming men as disciples bear this out. Your ministry with men will be a reflection of the leaders God raises up within your parish. This chapter will help you gather and train leaders to sustain a vibrant ministry to men in your parish.

IF YOU VISIT Amazon.com and enter "leadership" in the search box, you'll find over 18,500 books available. Why are there so many titles? Perhaps it is because everyone recognizes the importance of leaders. Or maybe it's because nobody seems to be able to get it right, so they keep buying more books about it.

This book may not be listed under "leadership" in the bookstore, but make no mistake: Leadership is the foundation of an effective disciple-making ministry. Nothing else you do will make any long-term difference without effective leadership. Without committed, involved leaders, it all falls apart. Leadership envisions, focuses, organizes, communicates, encourages, equips, perseveres, and celebrates. A ministry built on any other foundation simply will not work.

FOUNDATIONS FOR MEN'S MINISTRY THAT DON'T WORK

Some leaders have tried to build their men's ministry on emotion. Reading the statistics we presented at the beginning of this book can energize a leader to want to make a difference! But emotion is not faith. Emotion will only carry you through a disappointment or two, and in men's ministry it doesn't take long to experience a lot of disappointment. Plus, guys can be put off by passion when it's not expressed in a healthy way. It can come off as, well, a little weird. No one wants to follow weird.

Some parishes try to build their ministry on obligation. They find a few well-spoken guys who show up for everything and then convince them that the men's ministry is very important. A little guilt works well here. Just remind potential leaders that God calls us all to serve the kingdom and you know just the place for them. Your plan for the men in your parish and community is simple: They just need to understand what the Church teaches and then do it. Attend Mass faithfully, come to the men's events, help out on work days, and raise well-behaved children.

As crazy as this sounds, many men's ministries are built on the foundation of one slightly overzealous man who wants to tell everyone else what to do. If that's you, please stop!

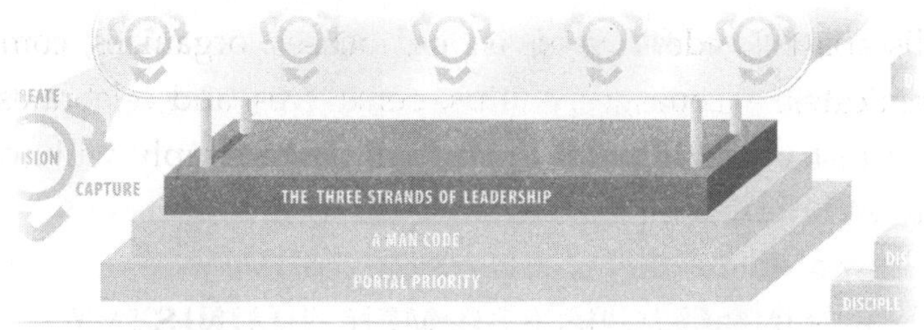

A WORD OF CAUTION

How long does it take for leaders to implement a successful men's ministry program? It takes a long time. Even Google, arguably one of the speediest success stories in corporate history, took over four years just to go live online. There really are no shortcuts. A "shortcut" takes years to develop.

Scholarly research indicates that, as a rule of thumb, about two-thirds of all program implementations fail. How does it happen?

Here are a few reasons:

- Leaders think they can wing it.
- They don't put in the time required.
- They underestimate how long it takes to make a disciple.
- They underestimate how long it takes to get a program going.
- They underestimate the resistance to change they encounter.
- They are not equipped.
- They don't get training because they think, "This should be pretty easy. How hard could it be?"

Every time a men's ministry fails, it's like a little inoculation. Just like a flu shot keeps the flu virus from being able to live in your body, the parish becomes more and more resistant to a sustainable men's ministry. The next leader who wants to build a men's ministry in the parish encounters increased resistance. After three or four such failed attempts, the parish's antibodies are fully developed and impenetrable. Men's ministry gets the reputation of a "loser." The pastor has decided, "That will never work here." Actually it will, but a made-up mind is almost impossible to change.

Research seems to indicate that unless a leader devotes at least five—and more likely ten—years to an initiative, success is unlikely. So unless you are willing to devote ten or more years to building a men's program, it would be better for the Catholic men's movement if you didn't start. These are serious times that require serious leaders willing to devote serious effort for a serious length of time.

If you are in the game for the long haul, here's the kind of leadership structure you should consider.

THE THREE STRANDS OF LEADERSHIP

Solomon wrote, "A threefold cord is not quickly broken" (Ecclesiastes 4:12). Your men's ministry will need three strands of leadership to reach its highest potential: 1) your pastor or another priest, 2) a primary leader for your men's discipleship efforts, and 3) a

The BIG Idea

The three strands of leadership for your ministry are the pastor, a primary leader, and a leadership team.

team of leaders to support him. You need the proper buy-in at each of these levels to have a well-balanced foundation.

You may be thinking, "But it's just me and the pastor carrying the ball on this right now. I don't have a leadership team." Or, "We've got a great team and a passionate leader, but our priest doesn't pay much attention to forming men as disciples." Or, "Our priest is behind us, but no one guy has really stepped up. We work by consensus."

Building your men's ministry without these three strands of leadership is like driving a car with a missing spark plug. The car will still run, but not like it should. It will sputter and misfire, lacking the power of an engine hitting on all cylinders.

LEADER STRAND #1: THE PASTOR'S ENTHUSIASTIC INVOLVEMENT

Tom was a lay leader in his parish. An accomplished businessman, Tom was adept at organizing and influencing. Luckily for his parish, Tom also had a heart for small groups.

For years Tom labored, with the blessing and public support of his priest, building up a small-group ministry in his parish. He prayed, recruited group leaders, oversaw training, organized curriculum, counseled, and worked his heart out. After seven years, he was able to build a small-group ministry in his parish with over one hundred adults each week.

When a Priest "Catches the Bug"

Then, one of the priests in his parish caught the small-group "bug." Suddenly, he realized how effective small groups could be for the spiritual development of his parishioners. So one spring, with the support of the parish council and Tom himself, the priest began a series of homilies about community and small groups. Over the course of several months, he laid out before the congregation the importance of relationships. He decided to cancel some of the normal activities and replace them with a designated "home group night."

That fall, the new initiative drew over seven hundred adults to participate in small groups.

Tom worked for seven years to build a small-group ministry with one hundred people. Then the priest sets a date, preaches a few sermons, reorganizes the schedule, and—voila!—seven hundred people get involved. Clearly, a priest's involvement is important.

Your pastor or parochial vicar will ultimately determine where the primary intellectual, financial, and spiritual resources of the parish are invested. If one of your priests is involved in a program or initiative, it will get a budget, staff support, rooms when it needs it, and plenty of publicity.

Support is not involvement. Research suggests that support of the ministry by a priest is good, but involvement is a lot better. If your pastor takes a personal interest in the process and health of your discipleship ministry with men, you have a huge head start.

This issue is one of the major complaints we hear from men's ministry leaders.

"Our pastor is just not behind us."

"Our pastor never attends our men's events."

"The men's activities barely get a mention at Mass."

That's ironic, because every priest wants to see his men become disciples. But many priests have been burned by men's ministry. In the past they have supported it, defended it, invested their time, and given it creative energy. But men's ministry didn't work. This was repeated for two, three, and maybe even four failed attempts.

If you were the pastor, and for the fourth time in eight years, some enthusiastic (or perhaps naive) guy excitedly said to you, "Father! I've got this great idea! We should start a men's ministry!" what would you do? You'd smile, and nod, and wish him well. Then you'd just wait.

This is not cynicism, just reality. A pastor is responsible to a multitude of constituencies—all of them wanting him to make their ministry his top priority.

Bringing the Pastor Aboard

So if your pastor or other priest does not jump on board at the beginning, that's OK. Be patient and persevere. There are also some ways you can help your pastor get involved in the men's ministry faster.

- *Pray for and with your priests.* Here's one idea: Gather your men on Sunday mornings before Mass and have a time of prayer for your pastor. Ask for specific requests. And don't just do it with the ulterior motive of getting him on board. Before even telling my men what I had in mind, I asked them to pray for me and my special intention as well as the pastor for a full month.

- *Support your priests.* The men's ministry leadership team needs to have a reputation of enthusiastic support for your priests. For example, discover your pastor's area of passion in ministry and rally around him to make him even more effective.
- *Inform your priests.* Your priests should never be surprised by what's going on in your ministry to men in the parish. For example, copy your pastor on your summary e-mails after meetings, and forward him stories of changed lives.
- *Include your priests.* Invite your priests and deacons to your events, but include them in the way they want to be included. A priest may not want to merely say the blessing or close in prayer; let him be one of the guys.
- *Love your priests.* Find tangible ways for the men's leaders to show your priests their appreciation.

A pastor, who is prayed for, supported, informed, included, and loved tangibly by his men will be much more likely to be involved in their efforts to grow closer to Christ. In fact, that pastor will want to participate in making that happen, throwing the full resources of the parish behind the effort. It will be good for your men, and good for your priests. (Turn to Appendix A for twenty-five more ideas for connecting with your pastor.)

LEADER STRAND #2: A PASSIONATE LEADER

An effective ministry to men needs a leader with an arrow through his heart for the men in your parish and community. Someone needs to wake up in the morning thinking, "How can I help the men in our parish to grow in their faith?"

Does he have to be a paid staff member? No. Could he be? It would be great if your parish or diocese paid a trained leader to devote a major portion of his time to men's ministry. If it's his only responsibility, that is even better. But for most parishes, the men's ministry leader will be doing it on a volunteer basis.

What other qualifications are there for the men's ministry leader? In a few minutes you could come up with a healthy list, but from our work these are the three most important attributes:

First, he should be a man who loves God. Your men's ministry leader should be modeling what he hopes other men to become: a disciple (follower) of Jesus Christ. He should be growing spiritually, spending regular time in prayer, and able to talk comfortably about his faith with other men. He doesn't need to be a Bible scholar or a great preacher or teacher. That's the priest's job. While your men's ministry leader needs to be actively seeking to grow in knowledge of his faith, he doesn't need to be a theologian.

Second, he should have a heart for men. Leaders in your parish have different passions and callings. The men's ministry leader must have a passion for reaching and forming men as disciples. And this needs to be his primary area of ministry in the parish.

Third, he should have the right set of gifts to lead other leaders. How can you tell? Look for a man who has the respect of other men. This does not necessarily mean he needs to be well known or popular. But frankly, there are too many men's leaders out there who are "self-selected." They have the passion but not the gifts. Be careful not to promote someone past the level of their competency as a reward for faithful service. Don't stop a man from ministering effectively where he is so that he can lead ineffectively in a new position.

LEADER STRAND #3: A COMMITTED LEADERSHIP TEAM

Surrounding the leader should be committed men who share many of the attributes of the leader himself. The height of your men's ministry will be determined by the depth of your leadership.

Q & A

Here's a radical question: Should we have non-Christians on our leadership team?

You may think this is a silly question. Of course, you're not going to ask this guy to take on a spiritual leadership role, but is there a better place for a guy who is seeking Christ than to be around Christian men who have a passion for discipleship? An earnest seeker who has been around for a while may help your leadership team understand the perspective of the men you are trying to reach.

Reflecting the Men You Want to Reach

Your men's ministry will become whatever your leadership team becomes. In other words, your leadership team should look like the guys you are trying to reach. If you want to reach men of different ethnic backgrounds, your leadership team needs to be ethnically diverse.

Everyone on your leadership team does not have to have the same level of spiritual responsibility or authority. Some members can play more of an implementation role while you are mentoring them for leadership. So, if you want to reach men at various levels of spiritual maturity, you might want to invite some guys at various places on their spiritual journey.

Encourage each leader to live his life in such a way that others can tell he has been "with Jesus" (see Acts 4:13). As a team, encourage the men to become to each other what they want their parish to become. That will create a model so attractive that other men will want to be part of it.

Involving Others and Staying Fresh

Finally, don't turn your leadership team into an "operations" or event committee. Your leadership team should be a prayer and strategic planning team, not a "doing" team. If you are planning a men's barbecue, then the leader who is responsible for the food should not decide on the menu, make a shopping list, buy the groceries, cook the food, and do the dishes. Rather, this is an opportunity to recruit men to these various tasks so they can begin to catch the vision. Bringing sodas is building the kingdom, but most men won't know that unless a leader shows them how their contribution reaches men with the gospel. (Again, that's casting the vision.)

We can't reiterate this point too strongly. If your leadership team is doing all the work, you can either disband now or wait a few years for it to fall apart. You may want to go ahead and make a tee time for Saturday because your ministry with men will not last unless you are constantly expanding the circle of men who believe in the vision.

Recruiting is hard work. It is often easier to just do it yourself. DON'T. DON'T. DON'T. If you want your ministry to last, constantly give away the work of the ministry to men who may become your future leaders.

One question we often hear is, "How big should my leadership team be?" You might be tempted to decide by thinking through potential areas of responsibility: A small-groups coordinator, a big-events coordinator, a retreat coordinator, and so on. Sounds pretty well-coordinated, doesn't it? But this approach is dangerous.

Men's leaders often tell us they are exhausted. It doesn't take long to discover they are trying to lead small groups and a retreat and coach a softball team and organize a bus to a men's conference and coordinate an outreach event and on and on. Why? Because they think that's what men's ministries are "supposed" to do.

This brings about two problems: First, they're burning themselves out. Second, nobody else wants to join the leadership team because they see how much work it is.

"The size of our ministry determines the size of our leadership team" is hazardous. Instead, look at it this way: "The size of our leadership team determines the size of our ministry." God has placed certain men in your parish with the desire to reach and disciple men. But for most of them it's not some vague calling; it's specific. Some feel passionate about softball, some about getting guys to go to men's conferences, some are into small groups, etc. Your ministry should flow out of the passions of your leadership team. If you don't have a guy who's passionate about retreats, then don't have a retreat. Believe it or not, "Thou shalt take thy men into the wilderness to retreat" is not actually in the Bible.

The men God has given you are not assets to accomplish the tasks set forth in your strategic plan. They are leaders. Their passions are wonderful clues to what God would have you do for the men of your parish. If you allow them to pursue their calling, they will be more engaged, your ministry will be more effective, and, best of all, more leaders will be attracted. Your ministry will grow naturally and in God's own time.

THE ARTT OF RECRUITING LEADERS

Recruiting leaders is a process. Here's a nice way to remember how this plays out in relationships: Appointment-Relationship-Trust-Task, or ARTT. How does this work?

Appointment

Create value for leaders by getting the appointment. The first time we saw our future wives, most of us didn't walk up and say, "Would you like to get married?" Instead, we asked for the appointment: a date for Friday night. So don't set your sights on a man and ask him to join your leadership team. Instead, ask for the appointment.

"Hey John, I'd really like to get your feedback about our men's ministry. How would you like to get together for coffee one morning?" The value for John is that you are asking him for feedback. If he really is a potential leader, he'll be happy to meet with you.

Relationship

During your appointment, start building a relationship. Tell him about your involvement and why it is important to you. Listen to his heart. But don't ask him to make a commitment to anything! Be satisfied with becoming his friend.

Trust

After you share your passion for men's ministry, be ready with a right next step. If he is indifferent, ask him how you can pray for him. If he is too busy to be more involved, offer to pray for him and ask him to pray for you and the men. If he is interested in going further, ask him to come to your next leadership team meeting as a guest. He can sit in and hear what's going on. Then you can meet again and talk about it.

By offering a next step that is appropriate to his level of interest and availability, you show him that you are interested in helping him fulfill God's mission for his life, not your mission for his life. Trust begins to develop.

Task

Trust is the key to actually doing something together. Once he shows an ongoing interest, then you can offer him a task—either through asking him to pray or to explore getting involved. Don't rush this process or you will scare away your potential leaders.

DOUBLE THE SIZE OF YOUR LEADERSHIP TEAM . . .

If there is one common complaint about leaders, it's this:

There are not enough of them. So here's an easy way to double the size of your leadership team.

Let's say you have four committed men on your leadership team. Make a covenant with each other to take one man to coffee or lunch each month and share why forming men as disciples is important to you. Use your "elevator speech" (see chapter eight). Follow this process for a year. Assuming each of you misses a month here or there, you will have conversations with at least forty men.

Your passion will not mean much to many of these men. Others will be glad for you but too busy to get involved themselves. But if just two out of every ten men express an interest in sitting in on a meeting (that means eight of your forty men), and half of those decide to get involved, you will have doubled the size of your leadership team in just a year!

. . . OR CUT YOUR LEADERSHIP TEAM IN HALF

It is hard work to build your leadership team. It is very easy to tear it apart. If your ministry is effectively forming men as disciples, your leadership team will be attacked by the Enemy. That's why it's so important that each member of your leadership team be accountable to other godly men. Every man needs someone who can look him in the eye and tell when something doesn't seem right.

Also, living in a fallen world means that leaders may be taken out of the game by events beyond their control. Family illness, a job transfer, or other circumstances may prevent a man from continuing on your leadership team.

But the quickest way to cut your leadership team in half is this: Try to sculpt a man into a better leader. It's a mistake to try chiseling away the ungodly parts of a man so that only the good stuff is left. It very rarely works that way.

Leaders need to be cultivated. Cultivation is an agricultural term. You cultivate a crop by choosing good seeds, preparing the soil, fertilizing it, and watering it regularly. Then you reap the harvest.

Leaders need to be polished, not chiseled. You polish leaders by encouraging them, not criticizing, and by affirming them, not correcting. Make sure your leaders have plenty of opportunities to be exposed to the love of Christ. If you want a better leader, help him become a better disciple.

Many times, you might think it is a good idea to "light a fire" under people. That is just plain wrong. The idea is to find people already on fire and just pour some gasoline on them.

THE HIGH CALLING OF LEADERSHIP

It is a high calling to be a part of a team of men who desire to disciple men. Our prayer is that God will use your team to raise up scores, hundreds, or even thousands of men who would be valiant warriors for Christ's kingdom.

To summarize, these are the three foundations of a sustainable disciple-making ministry to men in your parish:

- a philosophy of ministry that says discipleship is the portal priority
- an environment that communicates the proper man code to men

- a leadership strategy focused on three strands—your pastor, a leader, and your leadership team

As you establish the foundation for your ministry, the next step will be to define the process you want to engage men in. The wide-to-deep continuum illustrates the path to becoming a mature disciple. We'll show you how this works in detail in the next chapter, and show you what activities in the parish can help men along on this journey.

Remember This . . .

- Every time a men's ministry fails, it's like a little inoculation—your parish builds up a resistance to men's ministry that is harder to overcome.
- "A threefold cord is not quickly broken." These are the three strands of leadership necessary for your men's ministry: the enthusiastic involvement of the pastor or another priest, a passionate leader, and a committed leadership team.
- The pastor's tacit support won't mean a lot; his active support is OK; his enthusiastic involvement is best.
- The men's ministry leader should have a heart for God, a heart for men, and the leadership gifts necessary to lead other leaders.
- The height of your men's ministry will be determined by the depth of your leadership.
- The men of your leadership team should become to each other what they want the men of the parish to become.

- Leaders need to be polished, not chiseled. They don't need you to light a fire under them—they're already on fire. Just find a way to pour some gasoline on them, then get out of their way!

Talk About This . . .

1. What is the history of men's ministry in your parish? When you say "men's ministry," what impression does it give people who are not involved? How can good leadership help you overcome or build on this impression?
2. Does your pastor believe that the men of your parish—or at least the men's leaders—support and love him? What would you be willing to do to show him you are behind him 110 percent?
3. Are you feeling a little burned out on men's ministry? Have you started to notice your fellow leaders feeling the same way, or have you even already lost some? Why do you think this is? What can you do about it?
4. Take a few moments and list the names of the men currently involved on your leadership team. List the one or two things each of you is passionate about. Prayerfully consider whether these are the things God wants your men's ministry to focus on right now.
5. In chapter twelve you will develop a plan to recruit new leaders. Spend a few minutes brainstorming, and start a list of men with whom you might want to connect.

Pray About This . . .

Pray together as a leadership team:

- That your pastor and priests will not just support your ministry but personally become involved.
- That God will bless your pastor's efforts to reach men.
- That God will raise up a man—if he hasn't already—who is passionately committed to giving every man in your parish an opportunity to become a disciple of Jesus Christ.
- That God will help each member of your leadership team discern the role he has called him to in that effort.

7

AN ALL-INCLUSIVE MINISTRY TO MEN

If you have one hundred men in your parish, how big is your ministry? Sometimes our assumptions and paradigms limit us from seeing the bigger picture. This is certainly true of ministry with men. This chapter will dropkick a few common paradigms—and help you understand how your parish can maximize the spiritual impact of every interaction you have with every man.

A PARISH WAS HAVING its annual men's retreat. Men from the leadership team became a subcommittee and took on the task of organizing it. They set some goals:

- Reach out to men who didn't traditionally attend their events.
- Help men get to know each other on the retreat.
- Develop a follow-up strategy that kept men involved after the retreat.

They worked hard to promote the event. Many guys who registered were not very involved in the parish and had never been on a retreat before. They had team members speak on a very practical level about how being a Christian affected their everyday life. The talks were short and had plenty of discussion time afterward. In order to make the new men feel comfortable, they allowed the men to sit wherever they wanted during the sessions and discussions.

They had lots of fun and competitive activities. And they offered a follow-up activity for guys to get involved in—smaller groups of men who would meet for six weeks to go deeper into the issues raised by the event.

During the retreat, it seemed as though guys were really getting to know each other. The discussion times were robust. The activities were fun, and a lot of laughing and joking occurred throughout the weekend. At the end of the retreat, men signed up for the follow-up, including those men who had not been involved before.

A SUCCESSFUL RETREAT . . . OR NOT?

A week or two later, the entire men's ministry leadership team met, including the retreat planning team. The men's ministry team leader opened the meeting with a time to debrief the retreat. The planning team was excited to talk about their success and frankly eager for a few pats on the back. What they heard next blew them away.

"Well," said one of the leaders, shifting uncomfortably, "I guess I'll start. I have to say I was really disappointed in the retreat this year. I just feel like we wasted an opportunity."

"Yeah, me too," added another leader. "For instance, the speaker hardly talked about really spiritual things at all. He didn't teach from the Bible; he mostly spoke about his own experiences."

"And the discussion times . . ." another man began. "Every time we were with different guys. We should have assigned guys to groups of four and stuck with guys from those groups for the whole weekend. We could have met and prayed together and hopefully gotten into some deep issues."

There were other comments about the speaker, not enough Scripture, insufficient time for praying the Rosary, not enough time dedicated to adoration of the Blessed Sacrament and other "missed opportunities" from the retreat. The planning team was stunned. They had met every goal they had set for the weekend, yet the leadership team was ripping it apart. What went wrong?

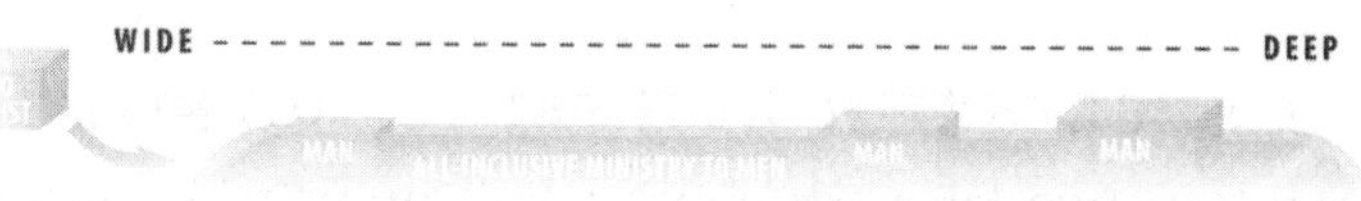

THE WIDE-TO-DEEP CONTINUUM

Making disciples is all about taking men where they are in their journey with Christ and helping them become mature, passionate followers of Jesus. This journey can be represented by a continuum:

MEN WHO NEED CHRIST - MATURE DISCIPLES

Your ministry to men will need to help men at every stage of this journey. We call this concept the *wide-to-deep continuum*.

WIDE - DEEP

Every man in your parish can be placed somewhere on the continuum, and that determines the offerings that will appeal to him. As a man matures in his faith, he will move further down the continuum.

How could knowledge of this continuum have helped the leadership team from the retreat example above? First of all, the planning team could have shared their goals with the rest of the leadership team and received their support and "buy-in" to the approach. All disappointment is the result of unmet expectations. The leadership team had one set of expectations about the target audience for the retreat; the planning team had another.

Notice that none of the suggestions that the other members of the leadership team made were bad. Teaching straight through passages of Scripture, staying with the same group of men for deeper discussions, having longer personal times with God—these are all great retreat activities to deepen men's faith.

But there was also nothing wrong with the type of retreat the team actually planned. It all depends on where you are aiming on the continuum.

APPLYING THE WIDE-TO-DEEP CONTINUUM

You will interact with men at all points along this wide-to-deep continuum. On the left, or "wide," side are men who are not all that interested in spiritual things. To reach guys on the wide side, you need activities that reach them at their point of interest. These are activities that require little or no preparation and low commitment. Typical activities at the wide end are softball teams, barbecues, a Super Bowl party, golf, hunting, or fishing.

To reach men on the "deep" side, you need activities that meet their spiritual needs more deliberately. These activities probably have a connection from week to week; they require preparation; they'll go deeper into spiriual concepts; they will offer accountability and transparency; and their focus will be on more mature Christians. Typical activities might include small groups, Bible studies, leadership training, service projects, or spiritual retreats.

> **The BIG Idea**
>
> Build a seamless process to move men across the wide-to-deep continuum.

No activity you plan can meet the needs of every man in your parish. In our illustration of the retreat above, the retreat planning team was focused on reaching guys more to the left of this continuum, while the rest of the leadership team was hoping for something reaching guys on the right of the continuum.

As you plan, make sure you are offering different types of activities to reach the different types of men in your parish. Build a seamless process to move men across the wide-to-deep continuum.

Also, be sure your leaders are clear about your target audience. Left to their own devices, your leaders will naturally tailor events to their passion and calling. Help them understand the purpose of the event so they can support the agreed upon agenda of the team.

LEADERSHIP TEAMS AND THE CONTINUUM

Different leaders will be passionate about reaching different types of men. As an example, consider the following hypothetical situation at your parish one Sunday morning.

Your men's ministry leadership team has just finished praying together before Mass. An usher approaches and tells your team that two men are in the vestibule asking for someone to talk to them.

One man has wandered in off the street. He is not sure why he is there, but he seems a little down and says that he is looking for answers. He wants to know what this Catholicism thing is all about. The second man has been involved in the parish for a while. Due to personal circumstances in his work and marriage, he really wants to take his relationship with Christ to the next step. He wants someone to talk with him about how to begin the next step on his journey with Christ.

Quick! You have to choose only one. Which man would you rather go talk with?

Some of you reading this book have a heart for evangelism. Your desire is to reach out to lost souls and point them toward the cross. Others are more drawn toward helping Christian men build the kingdom of God. You like to help men understand what it means to pray and grow in knowledge of their faith. When we present this scenario to men's leaders, about half of the leaders want to talk to the man who is seeking Christ for the first time while the other half feel drawn to talk to the man who is seeking a deeper relationship with Christ.

Think back to the continuum. Men at the left side of the continuum are seekers, trying to find their way to Christ. Men on the right side are leaders, wanting to follow Christ more closely and serve Him. Most leaders are wired to work with men at a certain point on the continuum. When you grasp this concept, it can help save a lot of trouble and misunderstanding.

After sharing this during a training course, a priest and the men's ministry leader from his parish came up and said, "You may have just saved our relationship."

The priest explained that he would go out into the community and meet new men and convince them to give the parish a try. But every time a new man walked in, his men's ministry leader would talk to them, invite them to join a small group, and explain the importance of accountability.

"As fast as I could get new guys in the front door," the priest said, "they were running out the back." Understanding the continuum helped the priest and the ministry leader realize that their hearts were focused on men at different places in their spiritual journeys.

The ministry leader learned that every man has to go through a process. They're not always ready for accountability and transparency. He and the priest agreed to develop an appropriate process to move men along the continuum.

THE WIDE-TO-DEEP CONTINUUM AND YOUR CONVEYOR BELT

The conveyor belt in our image includes all the activities and interactions your parish has with men. It's these interactions and activities that engage men and help them move forward in their spiritual journey. But it's a fallacy to think that all these interactions have to be men's-only activities, driven by the traditional idea of a men's ministry.

How Many Men Are in Your Men's Ministry?

Think about your parish for a moment. In the spaces below, write down the answers to these two questions:

How many men do you have in your parish? ____
How many men do you have in your men's ministry? ____

We ask this question at every training class we do in Orlando. While the answers may vary, we typically get answers like: 500 men, 50 in our men's ministry; 100 men, 20 in the men's ministry; 75 men, and we don't even have a men's ministry.

Who are the men you think of as being "in" your men's ministry? Is it the guys who come to your monthly men's breakfast? The twelve guys who gather on Wednesdays at six o'clock in the morning for Bible study? Is it the group of men who went on the last retreat?

We'd like you to consider looking at this concept differently: Everything your parish does that touches any man is men's ministry. Everything! So if you have one hundred men in your parish, the size of your men's ministry is one hundred. The only question is, "Is it an effective or ineffective ministry?"

As we said earlier, "Your system is perfectly designed to produce the results you are getting." We also said that your parish's ministry with men is perfectly designed to produce the men you have sitting—or not sitting—in your pews.

What would happen if you started thinking of your men's ministry in these terms?

- Every man in my parish is part of the men's ministry.
- Everything our parish does for and through a man is men's ministry.

An all-inclusive men's ministry tries to maximize the spiritual impact of every interaction with every man, no matter the setting. Singing in the choir, parking cars, working with the youth, doing volunteer accounting, or attending Sunday Mass—it is all ministry to and through men. The job of a leader is to determine how to help men be disciples in each of these contexts.

An All-Inclusive Mind-Set Solves Typical Problems

An all-inclusive view of your ministry to men helps eliminate the "us versus them" mentality that sometimes develops between men in the parish. Any growing parish has a group of men who are working hard every week in faithful ministry. Many of these men are simply unable to also be involved in your men's-only activities. It's foolish to imply that a deacon who spent two and a half hours installing a new dishwasher for a single mom is not part of the men's ministry because he does not get up at six thirty the next morning for a Bible study. These are exactly the kind of men we are trying to produce, and they are a vital part of what God is doing through the men of our parishes.

A parish shared one of its "problems." This parish was reaching lots of young fathers in the parish community through its family sports program. This often led to the men getting involved in marriage activities and children's events. Some of these men were beginning to serve in leadership positions in the parish. The leaders said, "We have a problem. We have these young men in our parish who were reached through our sports programs. Now they are serving as lectors, extraordinary lay ministers of the Eucharist, marriage preparation volunteers, and bereavement ministers, and they have never come to any of our men's ministry events.

> **The BIG Idea**
>
> An all-inclusive men's ministry maximizes the impact of every interaction with every man, no matter the seeting.

We restated it this way for them: "You have men in the parish community who were not strong in their faith. You reached them through your children's sports ministry. These men and their wives became connected with other families and the parish. They are growing as Catholics. They are becoming leaders and actually serving in various capacities in your parish. And the problem is . . . ?"

Together they were able to see that this really wasn't a problem at all. The only problem was that as leaders they had a stunted view of what constituted ministry to men.

If everything the parish does that touches men is men's ministry, then you have a vested interest in helping every ministry succeed. The other ministries in the parish should believe that the men, and the men's ministry leadership, are eager for them to fulfill the mission God has given them.

An all-inclusive men's ministry will leverage the efforts of the other ministries in the parish to help you achieve your purpose of forming men as disciples. Rather than reinventing a men's-only activity every time, throw your weight behind some events your parish has already planned that reach men. It's not appropriate for us to say to men, "We'll disciple you if you come to our activities or events." Jesus didn't say, "Come and be discipled." He said, "Go and make disciples." God is calling us to go where our men are and disciple them there.

As part of a men's leadership team, you don't have to do all the heavy lifting. Your parish is probably already doing things that are working to disciple men. Remember, every activity that reaches men is men's ministry. Take advantage of the classes, groups, and processes that are making male disciples in your parish. Help the leaders and men in these settings see them as opportunities to disciple men.

Support other events and ministries in the parish by adopting them as part of your ministry to men. For instance, as a men's ministry, offer to set up and break down for your next big ministry fair sponsored by the parish council or evangelization team. Offer to recruit the male volunteers for your children's ministry. Rally your men around the next work day sponsored by your grounds committee.

NOT ANOTHER DEMAND ON YOUR PRIESTS

An all-inclusive ministry mind-set leverages the work and contribution of your priests. Think about it. If everything your parish does that touches men is part of your men's ministry, then your pastor is the "tip of the spear," so to speak, of your efforts to disciple men. It will be a relief for your priest to know that you don't have to invent a whole new set of programs to have a men's ministry. Help him understand that your intention is for all the things your parish is already doing with men to become even more effective. Brainstorm with him how to make your parish more male friendly and how to support the leaders of other ministries. Getting your priests to think about how to disciple men in your parish may be the single greatest contributor to the success of your ministry.

UNEXPECTED LEADERS

Not just your priests benefit from an all-inclusive men's ministry approach. Just as important, we need to inspire other leaders in the parish to see every interaction they have with men as a disciple-making opportunity.

For example, just about every parish has ushers. If you were to ask the head usher in your parish, "What is the purpose of the ushers? Why are these men (or women) here?" he might say things like, "To serve people by making sure they know what's going on and helping them find a seat," or, "To help maintain a prayerful atmosphere throughout the Mass as people come in and out." In the end, his answer probably would boil down to handing out bulletins and getting people to sit down—the quicker the better.

What if you could inspire your head usher to a new vision: "Why are these ushers here? These men are here to become disciples of Jesus Christ." What would happen if he were able to see his primary role as helping disciple the other ushers, and only *secondarily* to get people seated? Here's an example that shows how you can do this:

Week One. The head usher tells all of the other ushers that he would like them to get there five minutes early next week. He has something he wants to share with them. He calls them all on Saturday to remind them.

Week Two. Five minutes earlier than usual, he gathers the ushers and hands them all two business cards—one is blank, the other has a Bible verse on it. He reads the verse to them and tells them why it is a meaningful verse:

"Now there are varieties of gifts, but the same Spirit; there are varieties of service, but the same Lord; and there are varieties of working, but it is the same God who inspires them all in every one" (1 Corinthians 12:4–6). Guys, this verse shows that everyone who serves is playing an important part. Our priests are serving God by celebrating the Mass, and we're serving the same God by helping people get bulletins and find seats. We're all an important part of a person's Sunday liturgy experience.

"Put this card in your wallet and pull it out this week when you have a minute. You may even want to memorize the verse.

"I'd like to pray for each of you, so on the blank card just write down your name and something you'd like me to pray about this week. Let me say a quick prayer now, and I'll collect the cards in a minute or two.

"Dear Lord, thank you for the opportunity to serve you this morning. Thank you for these men and women who are willing to give up their time to be ushers. Help us remember you as we go through life this week. Bless our families and our parish for your glory through Christ our Lord. Amen."

Weeks Three and Four. He does the same thing, but he starts to ask them if they have any thoughts about the verse and if there are any prayer requests they'd like to share with the group.

Week Five. This week the head usher only gives each person the card with the Bible verse. After he goes over it and they talk for a few minutes, he asks them to write their name and prayer request on the back of the card and trade with each other.

As time progresses, they meet a few minutes earlier to accommodate the discussions that have started happening. Different guys start praying. The head usher misses a week and asks one of the others to do the verse that week. Other people volunteer to bring a verse. Finally, some of them are enjoying the time so much they decide to start or join a small group.

When they started, the ushers thought they were just there to hand out pieces of paper and get people to sit down. With a process like this, it's likely God will help them move from serving out of a sense of obligation (or avoidance of singing during the liturgy) to serving out of the overflow of their relationship with him and each other. This is a step forward in their spiritual journey, moving them down the continuum. They are becoming better disciples.

Take a moment and think of all of the ways in which men are involved in the parish: serving as musicians, singing in the choir, acting as ushers and greeters, leading the Liturgy of the Word for children, serving as lectors or Eucharistic ministers, belonging to the Knights of Columbus, helping with youth programs, teaching RCIA, acting as parking lot attendants. How can you inspire leaders to reach these men where they are and help them become disciples of Jesus Christ?

EVERY MAN IS PART OF YOUR MEN'S MINISTRY

Finally, an all-inclusive men's ministry helps every man in the parish feel like he is a part of something bigger than himself. It allows each man to be involved in your parish wherever he feels God is calling him to participate.

If every man in the parish is part of our men's ministry, then we must come up with innovative and effective ways to communicate that message to, well, every man! (This is why the resonance and external slogan concepts coming up in chapter eight are so important.)

For instance, one parish calls its men's ministry Iron Men. To help every man feel a part of the men's ministry, they always refer to the men of the parish as iron men. If you go to church there—even for one week—you are an iron man. Almost every time there is an announcement to the men, whether it is in the service or elsewhere, the statement is made, "Every man in our parish is an iron man." Sound hokey? Perhaps, but when you look around the church on Sunday, you'll see the guys sit up a little straighter every time it is said.

Wherever men are involved, you need to "claim" them for your men's ministry in a way that supports and honors the other ministries of the parish. Help these committed men understand that coming to the annual men's retreat or monthly men's breakfast or weekly Bible study is not a requirement to be part of the men's ministry. The men working in the soup kitchen need to see themselves as a man in ministry. Provide them aprons with the logo of your men's ministry. This gives a dual benefit. First of all, the man looks down at that logo and says, "The men of this parish consider me a part of the men's ministry. They think what I am doing is important, and I've got the apron to prove it!" Second, others see the logo and say, "Wow, the men of this parish are willing to do whatever it takes."

Help men who assist with parking see themselves as men in ministry. Give them prayer cards each Sunday with the men's ministry logo, a Scripture verse, and a prayer request for the parish. Ask them to use any downtime to pray.

What other areas can you think of where men are already involved? How would you engage those men in discipleship and help them feel like they are part of the men's ministry in your parish? Think about men who serve or participate in:

- Teaching a religious ed. class
- Working on the sound system
- Running RCIA or adult faith formation classes
- Helping in the youth group
- Assisting with a building project
- Singing in the choir
- Coaching a children's team in a sports league
- Working with the Boy Scout troop

There is no end to the creative and unique ways you can help men feel like they are a part of what God is doing through the men of your parish. In the end, the message must communicate that it's not about a program that you want men to join. Help men feel like your parish values and desires that every man would learn to experience God's love and the brotherhood of other men.

The goal of your ministry to men is to create a system that moves men from wide to deep across this continuum. You have in your arsenal every interaction your parish has with every man. In the next chapters, we'll pull these concepts together into a system that moves the conveyor belt and connects these activities so that every man in your parish can become a passionate disciple of Jesus Christ.

Remember This . . .

- No single activity can meet the needs of every man in your parish. Where a man is in his spiritual journey will determine the kinds of offerings that appeal to him.
- Leaders need to agree on the target audience for a ministry activity or program.
- Having an all-inclusive ministry to men mind-set means:
    - Everything that your parish does that touches a man is men's ministry. Everything.
    - The size of your men's ministry is equal to the total number of men in your parish, plus every man you'd like to have in your parish.
    - You should leverage the efforts of the other ministries to help you achieve your purpose of forming men as disciples.
- Inspire other leaders in the parish to see every interaction they have with men as a disciple-making opportunity.
- Give men who are working in other ministries something to identify them as part of the men's ministry, even though they may be working in the soup kitchen, as an usher, or as a parking attendant.

Talk About This . . .

1. Where are you on your spiritual journey? Take a few minutes for each person on your team to tell his story.
2. What group of men do you feel most drawn to disciple? What

about other men on your discipleship team? Do they seem to be drawn toward one type of man? What difference will this make in terms of where you focus your efforts as a leader?

3. Brainstorm some of the activities men in your parish are involved in that are not "men's ministry." Does your parish battle an "us versus them" with these ministries? If so, what are some of the ways you can get beyond this?
4. List a few concrete steps your men's ministry can take to support the other ministries in the parish. How could you help them to disciple men more effectively? Is there an "unexpected leader" you could encourage with a vision for forming men as disciples?

Pray About This . . .

Pray together as a leadership team:

- That God would help every man in your parish to move forward in his spiritual journey.
- That God would help each of you find your calling (the unique way God has wired you to work with men) and maximize the impact you have on the men.
- That other ministries of the parish see that the men's ministry is as committed to their success as it is to its own.
- That your priests and deacons embrace the all-inclusive mindset and come to see their role as being the "tip of the spear" for your parish's ministry to men.

PART THREE

PLANNING AND EXECUTING YOUR MINISTRY TO MEN

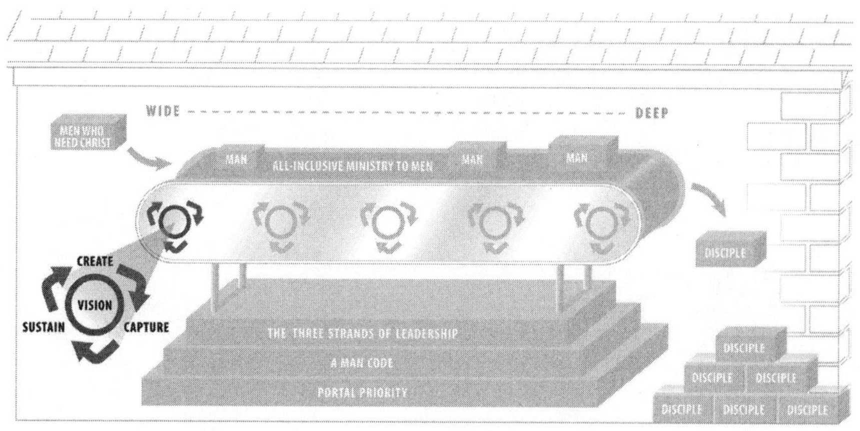

8

VISION: A COMPELLING REASON FOR MEN TO GET INVOLVED

Every conveyor belt has a motor that provides power to keep it moving. The power for your discipleship ministry with men is the Vision-Create-Capture-Sustain *strategy. We'll deal with these concepts in the next four chapters of the book. We begin with helping you instill a sense of mission and vision in the men of your parish.*

WOULD YOU DO US A FAVOR? Tap your foot while you read this section of the book.

Seriously. This is not just an academic exercise where you will get the point even if you don't actually do what we say. We really want you to tap your foot while you read the next few pages of this book. Go ahead. Feel free to move it very slightly so that people around you don't think you're weird. Just make sure you tap your foot up and down. Are you tapping? Good.

If you stopped a man in your parish on Sunday morning and asked why he was there, what would he say? You'd probably hear answers like, "Coming to Mass is the right thing to do"; "I want to make sure my family comes to Mass"; "I like to worship"; or, "I like the homilies." A particularly transparent man might say, "My wife wants me to come, and I don't want to make her mad."

What about some of the men who are more involved? If you asked an usher why he served, how would he answer? How about a man who helps park cars? Who sings in the choir? Leads a men's small group? Works with the middle school youth group?

(Don't stop tapping your foot yet. Trust us.)

Too often men go to Mass without any real sense of purpose. They participate in activities because they are supposed to, or because someone asks them to, but they don't really know why they are involved. Most of them have never been given a compelling reason why the Church should be a priority in their lives. They have never heard—in language they can relate to—that joining Christ in transforming the world is the adventure their hearts have always longed for.

FOR NO APPARENT REASON

Are you still tapping your foot? Let's assume this chapter kept going on and on and we never told you to stop. How long would you keep tapping? If you are a skeptical person, you might tap a few times and then quickly stop. If you are a particularly diligent person, you might keep tapping your foot for five or even ten minutes. But eventually every person who reads this book will stop. Why? Because you would realize you were tapping your foot for no good reason.

What if we said, "Tap your foot for ten minutes and we'll give you ten thousand dollars"? Almost any man would be willing to do that. Why? Because he understands the goal he is trying to accomplish. (We aren't giving you ten thousand dollars, so if you are still tapping your foot, you can stop now.)

Many men in parishes are "tapping their feet" with no idea why. They may continue to be engaged for a while, but eventually they'll get tired, bored, and discouraged. And then their spiritual lives will begin to grow cold, wither, and die.

These men know down deep inside that they were made for something more.

THE POWER OF VISION

The first step in building the right strategy is to formulate your vision. God desires for the parish to reach men with the gospel of Christ and help them grow to maturity. In the Great Commission (see Matthew 28:18–20), Jesus calls us to make disciples by sharing his message. In Ephesians 4:11–13, Paul teaches that God gives some people special abilities to equip others for works of service. Leaders, then, are called to disciple and equip people so they can do the actual work of the ministry and mature to become all God is calling them to be.

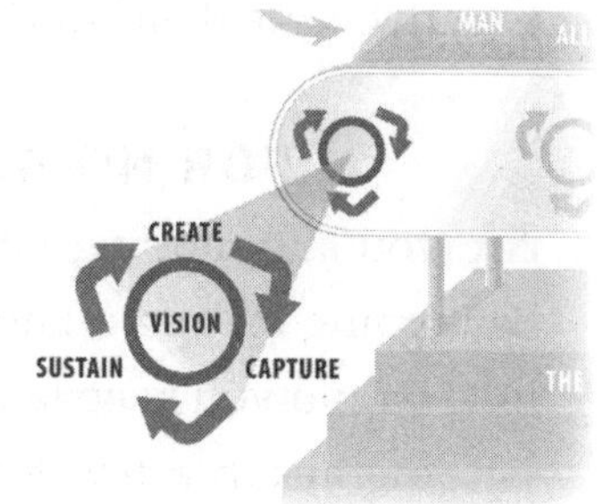

In the fourth century BC, Philip of Macedonia took control of several northern Greek cities. Down in Athens, the two greatest political orators of the day, Isocrates and Demosthenes, spoke out about the danger. They debated whether the men of Athens should attack Philip or wait and see if he attacked Athens. Isocrates, a teacher, made sure he presented the facts well. Demosthenes, on the other hand, concerned himself not only with what was "true," but also with what could be "made true" by the actions he advocated.

Needed: More Demosthenes

Both men addressed the threat that Philip presented. When Isocrates finished explaining why they should wait, people commented: "How well he speaks!" But when Demosthenes spoke about Philip's threat, they exclaimed: "Let's march against Philip!"

> **The BIG Idea**
>
> Ideas are more powerful than labor. Ideas set forces in motion that, once released, can no longer be contained.

We need more "Demosthenes" (men of action) in our interactions with the men in the parish. We have cheated men by obscuring the incredible adventure of changing the world through Christ behind programs and activities.

Ideas are more powerful than labor. Ideas set forces in motion that, once released, can no longer be contained. Here are some examples of important ideas expressed in a powerful manner:

- "We will put a man on the moon by the end of the decade." —John F. Kennedy
- "A computer in every home and on every desk." —Bill Gates
- "I want to make it possible for anyone in the world to be able to taste a Coke during my lifetime." —Robert Woodruff, CEO, the Coca-Cola Company, 1950s

Do ideas make a difference? Today you can ascend to the top of the highest mountains in Nepal or descend to the lowest elevation on earth, Death Valley, and what will you find? Empty Coke cans. Communicating the right idea in a compelling way is a powerful force.

If your announcements state that your "men's ministry will meet Saturday morning at 7:00 A.M. for breakfast and fellowship," that's a lie. It may be technically accurate, but it is a lie in every way that matters. Your men's ministry is not a meeting following some schedule of activities. Your men's ministry is about being part of what God is doing to transform lives through the men of your parish.

Men are tired of doing things "just because they should" or for no apparent reason. Men—especially younger men—want to be involved in something bigger than themselves.

Making It Resonant

If we said, "Just Do It," what images come to your mind? What about the slogan "Be All That You Can Be"? Both slogans work because the companies and organizations behind them have spent a tremendous amount of time, effort, and money reinforcing them to our hearts and minds. The words resonate with us.

Consider "Just Do It." There is nothing in those three words that mentions sports. The slogan could just have easily been adopted by a travel agency, a credit card company, or a job placement firm. But not anymore. Those words will now be owned forever by Nike.

> Such phrases resonate with millions of people around the world. How about your men? Are you communicating with them in a way that connects with them emotionally? We need to go beyond simply conveying information to our men. In most cases they don't need more information; they need God to awaken their hearts. Our job is to faithfully communicate in ways that stir the passion of our men for his glory.

A PROCESS FOR DEVELOPING YOUR VISION

The vision for your men's ministry needs to be in line with the overarching vision and the particular purpose of your parish.

Does your parish have a purpose, mission, or vision statement? If so, write it in the space provided or on another sheet of paper.

____

____

____

____

____

We will now help you formulate the vision of your men's ministry in three steps: as an *internal purpose statement,* an *external slogan,* and an *elevator speech.*

Step One: An Internal Purpose Statement for Your Men's Ministry

Does your men's ministry have a vision or purpose statement? Let's take some time right now to review or formulate one by thinking through some of the key ideas that should be included. We call this an *internal purpose statement* because it should be used mainly with your leadership team as an aid in prayer and strategic planning.

Two of our foundational principles are particularly important as you think about the vision of your men's ministry. First, remember that *it takes a long time to make a disciple.* Have a long-term perspective. Don't look for a quick fix in a few months. Instead, pray and plan for what God wants to do over the next five or ten years.

Second, *most meaningful change takes place in the context of relationships.* Men change as they interact with other men. Your men's ministry vision should include helping men develop meaningful relationships with other men.

You may want to have biblical themes and phrases reflected in your internal purpose statement. Consider the following Scripture passages (and others), and make notes of key ideas and themes that you would like to consider for your purpose statement: Proverbs 27:17; Matthew 28:18–20; Galatians 6:1–2; Ephesians 4:11–16; Colossians 1:28–29; Colossians 3:19, 21; 2 Timothy 2:2.

Not only should you be aware of what the Bible teaches about ministering to men, you should have a good handle on the practical needs of men in your parish community. It won't do you any good to design a men's ministry that won't actually reach any of your men.

Take a short break and spend about twenty minutes on the phone. Call one, two, or three representative men from your parish and community. Discover their needs by asking questions such as the following:

- "In what area of your life do you feel the most pressure?"
- "If our parish could do one thing for you, what would you want it to be?"
- "What is the most valuable experience you've had at the parish in the last year?"
- "What is the worst experience you've had at church in the last year?"

Note their answers in the space provided.

Now, prayerfully combine the thoughts and ideas generated by this material into an internal purpose statement for the men's ministry of your parish. Remember, a purpose statement basically says what you will do and how will you do it.

Whatever words you use, your purpose should have at its core Jesus' command to "make disciples."

Here's a sample men's ministry internal purpose statement: "To reach men with a credible offer of the gospel and equip them as transformational leaders for their families, parish, work, and the world." (See appendix B for more vision statement examples.)

If your men's ministry has a purpose statement, write it here. If not, write a sentence that captures the essence of what you believe God wants the men's ministry of your parish to accomplish.

____

____

____

____

Step Two: An External Slogan to Challenge Your Men

Next, it is helpful to have a slogan that resonates with the men in your parish. While your internal purpose statement charts a course, the external slogan helps recruit your team's Demosthenes! It doesn't change or add to your purpose statement but rather "distills" it to a simple, high-impact message. It can help make the vision clear, even powerful, to your men. It's how Kennedy, Gates, and Woodruff captured people's imagination.

When men hear your slogan, you want them to remember the compelling ministry being accomplished for and by your men. A slogan is like a plastic bag at the grocery store. You don't go to the store to get a bag; the bag allows you to carry all your items home. A slogan or phrase that resonates is like an empty bag that you fill with the content and experiences that support the vision and mission of your parish. After a few years, men who hear your slogan will automatically think about the incredible mission trip to Mexico, the amazing outreach event in your community, the day they reroofed the widow's house, or the way their group helped a man through his marriage crisis.

How will you call men to go with you on this adventure? Bruce Barton once said, "Jesus brought forth man's best efforts not with the promise of great reward, but of great obstacles."

Develop a resonant phrase or slogan that lets your men know you are playing for keeps. Call men to join a great vision of what God could do in your midst. Inspire them to join a cause that literally means the difference between eternal life and death for hundreds and thousands of men and their families.

Look for a short, visual, concrete, memorable statement that resonates with men. Make it action-oriented, rather than descriptive. Imagine what it was like for rural fishermen to hear Jesus' call to "make disciples of all nations"!

After attending our Leadership Training Center, one leader took his accurate, precise, and completely boring purpose statement and turned it into "Training Men for the

Battle." The Lord has used this (and other truths he learned) to give new power for his ministry to men.

Here are some sample slogans: Building Iron Men; Brothers in the Great Adventure; Every Man a Disciple; Reaching Men, Exalting Christ. See Appendix B for more examples.

Use the space below to try out several slogans; then provisionally pick the best one.

____

____

____

____

____

In addition, many leaders have found it helpful to have a resonant name for their men's ministry. The right name gives your ministry an identity that is compelling and inviting. Here are some sample names: Men of Faith; Iron Men; Band of Brothers; Men of Valor. (Once again, additional ideas can be found in appendix B.)

Use the space below to brainstorm names. Try them out with your slogan. For example: "Men of Faith—Brothers in the Great Adventure." (You'll finalize your name, slogan, and internal purpose statement in the exercises in chapter twelve.)

____

____

____

____

____

Step Three: Your Elevator Speech

Train your leaders to share their passion for your men's ministry with other men. Help them develop a four- or five-sentence explanation about why they are excited about what God is doing through the men of your parish.

This is called an "elevator speech." Imagine you are getting on an elevator and one of the men from your parish walks on as the doors are closing. He says hello and then asks, "I know you are involved in the men's ministry at church, and I've been thinking. Why should I get more involved?" He then pushes the button for the fifth floor and you have less than a minute to convince him. What will you say?

Begin training your leaders to give their elevator speech by working on a short script that contains:

- *The Introduction.* For example, "Eddie, I'd love to quickly share with you what God is doing in our ministry to men."
- *The Vision.* "As you may know, we are training men for the battle. Nothing has the power to change the world like reaching men . . ."
- *A Success Story.* "I don't know if you've met Jose Aguilar yet, but he has a great testimony of how God is working. Ted Rogers invited him to our communion breakfast last fall and Jose joined a small group. Now Jose and his wife have become very active in our parish. It fires me up to think that his three precious children have a whole new future ahead of them with a godly dad."

- *A Next Step.* "We have some great ministries going on right now—small groups, service projects, and our annual retreat. Also, if you'd like to sit in on one of our leadership meetings, we'd love to have you join us as our guest. Our next meeting is a week from Sunday. Would you like to come?"

Here's a real-life example. A member of the leadership team had invited a man to join his men's ministry leadership team. After the first meeting, his friend expressed doubt about whether he wanted to be involved. It seemed like meetings and activities. What was the men's ministry really trying to accomplish?

They had both just witnessed a man in their small group who abandoned his wife and teenaged kids for another woman. The leader was ready with an elevator speech:

"Bill, do you remember what happened with Rob? You and I sat next to him for six months in our small group. Did you have any idea something was going on?"

"No," he said sadly. "I didn't."

"Me neither. And that's why we need a men's ministry. Every man in our parish needs another man who can look him in the eye and tell when something's wrong."

In a flash, Bill "got it." He literally slammed his hand down on the table. "I want to be a part of that!"

Take a few minutes and write an elevator speech that quickly explains your vision for men's ministry in your parish in the space below. Use the "Introduction, Vision, Success Story, Next Step" outline. Time your presentation to make sure you can tell the story in about sixty seconds.

Share your elevator speech with other men as often as you can. Have your emcees use their version at each of your events. Use it when you invite men to participate in activities, events, or groups. Use it when you meet potential leaders. Keep your vision in front of as many men as possible, as much as possible.

BE VISION-FOCUSED RATHER THAN EVENT-CENTERED

An external slogan helps you constantly remind your men that you are doing things for a reason. Too often, local parish men's ministries have been driven by events rather than vision. We schedule events—like a monthly men's breakfast or annual retreat—and before long men perceive that the events are the ministry. We become discouraged when men don't attend events because that is how we measure the effectiveness of our ministry. Yet often men don't come because there doesn't seem to be any larger purpose to the events.

If we are not careful, we can "begin" without really knowing where we want to "end." It is easy to get caught up in the breakneck pace of men's ministry and "event" yourself to mediocrity.

Every event that you schedule as a part of your ministry to men should serve your overall vision. At the event, explicitly communicate to the men how this event fits in the larger context of your ministry and the vision of the parish. Explain what you hope to accomplish and how it contributes to your overall goals. Use your external slogan over and over to reinforce this vision.

BE POSITIVE, NOT NEGATIVE

Men want to respond to a challenge. They don't want to be yelled at. Make sure you formulate a vision with a positive agenda about what God can do rather than a negative rebuke about how badly men are doing. Men don't respond well when we talk down to them. Use a positive approach to draw men toward the great calling God has given them, rather than berate them to leave lesser things behind.

It would be impossible for us to overemphasize the importance of developing and sharing the vision for your men's ministry (using the internal purpose statement, external slogan, and elevator speech). It is the single most important ingredient for creating the kind of atmosphere God uses to change men's spiritual lives.

Remember This . . .

- Most men today feel bored and left out of their parish. They are tapping their feet. Are your men tapping theirs? Why not call them to something great and see how they respond?
- Men are tired of doing things "just because they should" or for no apparent reason. Men want to be involved in something bigger than they are.
- Your vision should be a resonant call to action, a compelling challenge, and a promise that men will go someplace worthwhile.
- Your vision for the men's ministry has three components:
    - An internal purpose statement. This answers what you will do and how you will do it.
    - An external slogan. This is the public face of your men's ministry and should make men say, "I want to be a part of that!"
    - An elevator speech. Every leader should be equipped with a sixty-second explanation of the vision of the men's ministry, why a man would want to be involved, and an invitation to do something.
- Every event that you schedule as part of your ministry to men should serve your overall vision. If it doesn't, cancel it.

Talk About This . . .

1. Men want to be a part of something going somewhere. How have you been frustrated in the past by being part of a group that seemed to lack direction and vision?

2. Are you presenting the men of your parish with an opportunity to belong to something bigger than they are? Think of the last few events your parish held for men. Did you place those events in the context of a larger vision? Did you communicate that larger vision to men when you announced or invited men to the activity? How can you improve this for upcoming activities?
3. On a flip chart or whiteboard, draft or refine your men's ministry internal purpose statement based on input from your pastor and each other. Use the work you did while reading this chapter. Draft an internal statement as a group and write it in the space below.

___

___

___

4. Effectively calling men to participate in the discipleship process will require you to capture their attention and challenge them to grow. Pick one of your slogans, fine-tune it, and write the statement in the space below. Then pick your ministry name and do the same thing with it. Take some time to discuss how you will use it.

___

___

___

5. Allow each man on your leadership team to share his elevator speech. Make suggestions for how you can begin to share these with other men.

Pray About This . . .

Pray together as a leadership team:

- That God would inspire your team and give you a compelling vision for your men.
- For guidance as you develop tools to communicate this vision.
- That God would help men clearly see the great adventure of following Jesus Christ.

9

CREATE MOMENTUM BY PROVIDING VALUE

After you've defined a vision and begun to communicate it consistently, how do you get men to start moving on their spiritual journey? The key to helping a stationary man get moving is to create value for him. Know your men, and then reach them in ways that are relevant to their lives. This chapter will help you know how to effectively create momentum with all your men.

ONE BENEFIT OF LIVING in central Florida is our proximity to Cape Canaveral, where they launch space shuttles. It's pretty amazing to see this mammoth machine strapped to external rocket boosters and a huge fuel tank, sitting on its tail pointed toward the sky. The voices of the controllers are calm and measured as they tick off checkpoints on the countdown to zero.

"Ignition!" Steam starts to escape and then smoke starts billowing. The shuttle shudders for a moment or two and then—barely perceptibly—it begins to lift off the pad. At first it moves so slowly, you almost expect it to fall over. After all, once it leaves the ground, it's basically sitting on the hot gases from the rocket engines. And then, "The shuttle has cleared the tower." Now it is definitely going up, moving faster and faster. Within minutes, it is traveling 17,000 miles per hour. From a hundred miles away, spectators can see the bright flame as it rises in an arc toward orbit.

The shuttle's external fuel tank is enormous. It holds 500,000 gallons of rocket fuel, which all burns up in about five minutes. Then the shuttle travels another four million miles on a little bucket of fuel.

The greatest amount of energy required in nature is that amount required to overcome inertia and put a stationary object—like a space shuttle—into motion. Overcoming spiritual inertia is the same way. We are surrounded by men who are spiritually stationary.

TWO COMMON TRAITS OF MEN

Men exhibit two common traits: Some are busy, and some are tired. Most are both!

There is a tremendous volume of noise in our lives. We live in a world of fast career tracks, high-speed Internet connections, and easy credit. All week long men are being bombarded by the media, their coworkers, their bosses, their family—everybody wants something.

No wonder it is rare men take time for spiritual self-examination. Many attend Mass only out of obligation, if at all. Others invest themselves in church hoping to feel needed and successful. See if you recognize either of these hypothetical men:

John attends Mass because he feels it is something he should do for his family. His wife really wants him to go to Mass, and he agrees with her that it is a good idea for his kids to receive some moral and religious instruction (as well as the sacraments). He goes through the motions—attending Mass, sending the kids to religious education classes, putting an envelope in the basket—but he's not actively pursuing a relationship with Jesus Christ. So he goes, but mostly to watch, not to participate. John is a tourist at Mass. He enjoys the experience while he's there, but then he goes home and life gets back to normal.

Frank, on the other hand, loves Mass. It makes him feel needed, like he is making a contribution. He attends faithfully every Sunday and serves on several committees and boards. He keeps saying he'd like to be more involved with men, but he's not in a small group, nor does he seem to have any true friends in the parish. When he's invited to join a men's event or go on the men's retreat, he regretfully declines because he's "too busy."

John and Frank are both cultural Catholics. Even though they look different from the outside, on the inside they are virtually identical. They are spiritually stationary. They are focused on themselves. A huge challenge for leaders is to get guys like John and Frank out of the comfortable patterns they use to stiff-arm God. (Of course, we face just as big a challenge with guys we would like to attract who aren't in our parish at all.)

Ironically, both John and Frank would likely respond if presented with a compelling challenge.

Discipleship is a spiritual journey, and as the saying goes, "A journey of a thousand miles begins with the first step." So how do we get men to take that first step—or for some, the next step—in this spiritual journey? In the last chapter we discussed step one: clearly communicating a compelling vision for your men's ministry. What's next?

OFFERING SOMETHING OF VALUE

Engage a man's attention by offering him something he will find valuable. Tired men need to believe that getting involved will be worth the effort. Busy men need to believe that of all the opportunities clamoring for their time, the one you are offering them is top notch. In short, you have to show them the value of getting involved.

> When you create value with an activity, you create momentum, the first gear that propels the conveyor belt of your discipleship process.

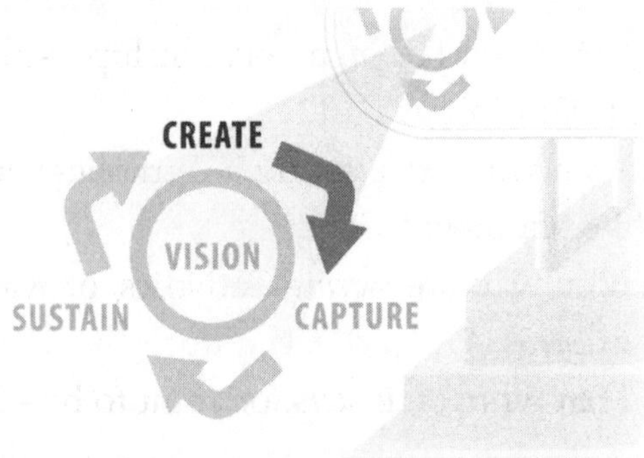

Often, we provide value for men with some kind of experience or activity: a Catholic men's conference, the men's retreat, or a barbecue. But it doesn't have to be a big event. Often the most valuable thing to a man is some personal one-on-one time, like inviting him to breakfast or lunch. Look for anything that compels a man to take a step forward in his spiritual journey.

There is no shortage of activities for men today. A little analysis will give you the insights you need to get your men's attention. You'll need to answer these two questions:

- What types of men are we trying to reach?
- What kinds of things will interest them?

KNOW YOUR MEN: FIVE TYPES

As you devise a strategy to create momentum among your men, you will want to take some time to categorize the men in your parish—perhaps by age or life situation. Below is Man in the Mirror's typology that churches use to help target their efforts. Every man in your parish fits into one or more of the following five categories:

- Type 1: Men who *need* a relationship with *Christ*—Romans 6:23; 1 John 5:11–12
- Type 2: Men who are *unengaged* Catholics (men on the "fringe")—Matthew 13:22
- Type 3: Men who are *mature* Catholics, or want to be—Matthew 13:23
- Type 4: Men who are *leaders*, or want to be—2 Timothy 2:2
- Type 5: Men who are *hurting*—Galatians 6:2

Type 1: Men Who Need Christ

These are men who are not Christians and know they aren't. Few if any of these men go to Mass. You will need to reach outside of the parish to pull these men in.

Take a few moments to think of men connected to your parish who may need Christ. What do these men look like?

- A man who comes occasionally with his family (think Christmas or Easter)
- A neighbor or coworker someone brought to the men's barbecue or Super Bowl party
- Guys who play on the parish softball team or show up for "Friday night basketball" in your parish gym
- A man who comes to the Christmas play
- A man who comes when his children perform in children's choir or to Catholic school events featuring his children
- A man who attends Ash Wednesday service to receive the ashes on his forehead or on Palm Sunday to get his palm branch for the year.

Picture these men in your mind. Write down their names. How would you describe them?

____

____

____

Type 2: Men Who Are Unengaged Catholics

These men come in two flavors: John and Frank (from our story earlier in the chapter). If you are a leader, these are the guys who probably frustrate you the most. They often seem poised to engage, telling you what you want to hear, but then backing out at the last second.

John is typical of men on the periphery of the parish. He may attend Mass fairly regularly, but isn't involved much beyond that. There are many men either just inside or outside the doors of the parish.

Frank, on the other hand, is very involved, but he uses his busyness at the parish to keep others at arm's length. He may at one time have had a vibrant faith, but the work of the parish has overwhelmed his love for Christ. Many people know who Frank is, but nobody really knows Frank.

The only way we've seen men like John and Frank be reached is through other men who take a personal interest in their lives. This can be difficult, because Frank will likely brush you off the first few times. Don't get annoyed. Just keep trying. Eventually, when they're ready, they will open the door to a deeper relationship. Make sure someone is there to take advantage of the opportunity!

Picture these men in your mind. What are their names? Describe them in your own words.

Type 3: Men Who Are Mature Catholics, Growing in Their Faith

These men are the "bread and butter" of your ministry. These guys, especially those early in their spiritual journey, are eager to develop their faith. Some are actively engaged, while others are waiting for someone to show them what to do.

Three things have special appeal to these types of men: learning, serving, and leading. First, they learn by responding to opportunities to serve in the parish, study the Scriptures and develop their faith. That's why these men fill small groups and adult education classes. Second, once mature Catholics get a taste of serving—at the homeless shelter or doing yard work for a widow, for instance—they often get turned on and will keep coming back. Finally, these are your candidates to begin exploring leadership. They'll join an officer training class or be willing to fill in for a missing usher or a sick Sunday school teacher.

It is easy to take these men for granted. After all, they pretty much do what you ask them to. They respond to the announcements, sign up at the table outside after Mass, and show up for the work project on Saturday morning. Of course, they make up a much higher percentage of the guys who show up for men's activities. But beware: You must challenge these men to keep growing. Bored men—even mature Catholics—are easy targets for distraction and sin. Be on the lookout for men who are "tapping their feet."

Are there specific men that came to mind as you read about mature Catholics? Picture these men in your mind. What are their names? Describe them in your own words.

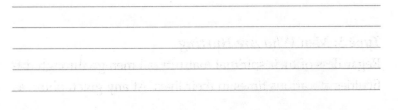

Type 4: Men Who Are Leaders

Right now you're probably thinking: Oh boy, do I wish we had more leaders! You may have more than you think. A leader is anyone who takes responsibility to get something done and influences others to join him in the effort. Once a man begins to be concerned about reaching and discipling other men, he has become a leader.

The men on your ministry teams and committees are leaders, of course. The guys who lead small groups and teach adult faith formation classes are obviously leaders as well. But so is the head usher, the captain of the softball team, the youth worker who mentors a boy with no dad, the man who sets up chairs each week, and other unseen and unexpected leaders.

You may think you don't really need to create value for these men. "They're already involved. They've bought into what the church is trying to do." Yes, but they are often busy and tired too. These men need you to consistently help them remember why they got involved in the first place.

Who are the leaders in your parish? Write down the names of the "expected" and the "unexpected" leaders. How would you describe these men? Are they excited? Tired? What do they need?

____

____

____

Type 5: Men Who Are Hurting

Regardless of their spiritual maturity, all men go through difficulties at various times in their lives. At any given point, as many as half the men in your parish may be going through marital problems, financial issues, struggling with a wayward child, involvement with Internet porn, dealing with the loss of a job, or struggling with the health crisis of a loved one.

What are the two or three most significant issues facing your hurting men? Could these men get help in your parish? Make sure you are supporting men in a way that makes it realistic for them to ask for help. There was once an actual announcement in a church bulletin that went something like this: "Men, are you struggling with feelings of depression because of financial or marriage problems? Sometimes it helps just to have someone to talk to. Call our counseling center to make a confidential appointment today at 555-1234. Ask for Susan." While this is a great announcement telling guys that it's OK to ask for help, very few men will call a stranger named Susan.

In training classes, men were asked to consider the proportion of these groups in their parishes. Included in the table below is the basic range of answers. What about your parish? Estimate your own numbers, both in percentages and in real numbers. At the end of the chapter, you'll use this information to evaluate your current efforts to reach men.

Level of Spiritual Development in Our Parish

Our Parish	# of Men	% of Men	Sample Churches
Men Who Need Christ	_____	_____	1–15%
Unengaged Catholic Men	_____	_____	35–70%
Mature Catholic Men	_____	_____	10–40%
Leaders of Catholic Men	_____	_____	5 –15%

FIGURE 7

THE FIVE TYPES OF MEN ACROSS THE CONTINUUM

Let's take a look back at the wide-to-deep continuum from chapter two. If you were to place each type of man across the continuum at the point that best describes him, it would look like this:

Type 1:	Type 2:	Type 3:	Type 4:
Need Christ	**Unengaged**	**Mature Catholics**	**Leaders**

WIDE - DEEP

Note: Type 5: Hurting men are in each of the other four groups.

The wide-to-deep continuum serves as a metaphor for a man's spiritual development. As a man moves forward in his spiritual journey toward Christ, he moves down this continuum as well.

The continuum is a helpful planning tool. There is no such thing as a one-size-fits-all men's activity. It's important to take into account what group of men you are trying to reach with any event you are planning for your men.

Choosing Activities Across the Continuum

Figure 8 shows a continuum drawn with the four types of men labeled so that it forms four columns. (Remember, there are hurting men in each category.) The chart is entitled "Men's Ministry Activities by Type." Under each type of man, make a list of the kinds of activities you think each type of man might enjoy. To get you started, we've put in several examples. Add your own ideas in the blanks provided.

Level of Spiritual Development in Our Parish			
Type 1: **Need Christ**	Type 2: **Unengaged**	Type 3: **Mature Catholics**	Type 4: **Leaders**
WIDE -- DEEP			
Sports/outdoor activities	Seminars	Retreats	Leadership training
Events involving his children	Adult education	Small groups	Accountability groups
	Service projects	Mission trips	

FIGURE 8

Managing Your Expectations

The continuum can also help you manage expectations. One year, a parish of about eight hundred invited Man in the Mirror to conduct a *Success That Matters* seminar. Over 120 men attended the seminar. The follow-up was very well received, and the seminar created a lot of momentum.

The next year, the same parish did another seminar, and this time one of the authors of the original book (*No Man*

Left Behind) was called on to conduct *Leading a Mission-Driven Life.* He arrived and met with the members of the leadership team, who were a little downcast. They only had seventy-five men registered for the event and couldn't figure out why. But things were better than they thought.

He drew a picture of the continuum on a whiteboard, and after a brief explanation of the types of men, asked the leaders how many of their men fit into each group. He wrote their answers on a whiteboard. They determined that of the about 350 men in their parish, 230 either were men who need Christ or unengaged Catholics; the remaining 120 were either mature Catholics or leaders. He then explained that the *Success That Matters* seminar is targeted for those guys who need Christ or are on the fringe. The marketing material focuses on men trying to balance work, marriage, kids, hobbies, finances, and recreational interests. It asks the question, "Have you ever thought, 'There's got to be more to life than this'?" Out of the 120 men who attended that event, about eighty men needed Christ or were unengaged Catholics. The other forty were mature Catholics or leaders.

But *Leading a Mission-Driven Life* is targeted more toward mature Christians or leaders. On the continuum, *Success That Matters* falls closer to the wide side; *Mission Driven Life* falls farther to the deep side. So the seventy-five men coming to the current seminar represented over half of the target group for this event! In other words, even though the total number in attendance was lower, the percentage of men in the target group was actually higher.

At the end of the meeting, the chart looked something like this:

800 People and 350 Men			
Type 1: **Need Christ** 5%=20 men	Type 2: **Unengaged** 60%=220 men	Type 3: **Mature Catholics** 25%=85 men	Type 4: **Leaders** 10%=35 men
WIDE - DEEP			

Total of 230 out of 350 men	**Total of 120 out of 350 men**
YEAR ONE	**YEAR TWO**
"Success that Matters"	**"Leading a Mission Driven Life"**
Target: Fringe	Target: Mature Catholics/leaders
Attendance: 120 men	Attendance: 75 men, almost all mature Catholics/leaders
Number in target audience: 80	Number in target audience: 80
Approx. 25% of the primary target audience	Over 50% of the primary target audience

The *Leading a Mission Driven Life* event reached a higher percentage of the target market. In other words, it may have been unrealistic to expect 120 men at the *Leading a Mission Driven Life*—and perhaps they should have had even more men the previous year! This analysis helped them manage their expectations about how many men should come to an activity. It could help you too.

IF YOU WANT MEN TO COME, YOU HAVE TO ASK THEM

Get ready. You are about to read a foolproof "marketing plan" to get the men of your parish to come to your next event. Ready?

First, create a four-color flyer for your event with cutting-edge graphics and hand it out to every man. After every Mass, pass out notices to each man announcing the event. Then make an animated PowerPoint presentation to show on the screen before every Mass starting two months before the event. You'll need to run some radio advertisements on the local Christian stations. Next, go out and purchase at least one billboard on every major artery leading to your parish to advertise your event. Go to the local airfield and pay for a skywriter so that the week before your event men can look up and see "Men's Barbecue Next Friday" written in the sky. Finally, slip your pastor a Starbucks gift card to announce it from the pulpit. Everybody knows that if the pastor tells men what to do, they'll do it.

OK, so by now you've realized that the plan above is not only a little expensive, but probably not effective either. It's just a formula for getting the guys to come who were going to attend anyway.

The Power of a Personal Invitation

> If you want new men to come, you must add one strategy to your promotions: *personal invitations*. All of your flyers, announcements, and PowerPoint slides accomplish one thing: They make it more likely that a man will say yes when *someone asks him to go*.

It makes sense, doesn't it? Think about how most Catholic men come to a personal relationship with Christ. They don't drive down the street, and see one of those "God billboards," and go, "Wow. I need to become a 'good Catholic' and ask Jesus Christ to be my Lord and Savior." They don't say, "I'm going home and watching as much EWTN as I can." No! Someone introduced them or reintroduced them to their Catholic faith and spent time reflecting the gospel to them by the Catholic life they led, and then asked them if they would like to walk a closer walk with Christ in their own life.

According to surveys by Religion in American Life, only 2 or 3 percent of people attended churches because of advertising, while 85 percent went after being invited by a friend or relative. Most catechumens and candidates entering RCIA are there because they have been invited by a friend to come learn a little more about the Catholic Church. Men need to be invited—personally. They will come to something with a friend that they would never come to alone.

From Zero to Fifty

In one parish the leadership team decided to host several events to build community among their men. The first was a father and child activity day. They put announcements in the bulletin, sent e-mails, and even had the pastor mention it from the pulpit. And when Saturday came, the leadership team gathered to greet and serve the men and children coming.

They waited. They waited some more. In the end, besides themselves, exactly nobody—zero men—came. (They were thinking about applying to *Guinness World Records* for the least successful parish men's event.)

The next event scheduled was a bowling night in January. Though a bit dispirited, they decided to go through with their plan. One of the leaders had suggested making the bowling night a competition. They recruited eleven captains who were each responsible for inviting four other men to be on their team. The night of the event, fifty-four men showed up, the most they had ever had for this type of men's activity. (They gave bonus pins for team members who did not attend Mass regularly—and had eleven unchurched men at the event.)

Why did it work? They only had to sign up eleven men for the event, and then those eleven went out and personally recruited the other forty-three. If you want men to come, personally invite them.

GIVE MEN WHAT THEY NEED IN THE CONTEXT OF WHAT THEY WANT

How do you reach men on the fringe without being "preachy"?

One Bible teaching model is, "What do men need to do?" Man in the Mirror's model has been, "What do men need that they are willing to do?" In other words, if a man needs to consider twenty areas, but he is only far enough along in his spiritual journey to engage in three of those areas; it doesn't make sense to talk about the other seventeen. Instead, focus on the three, lead him along, then add other subjects as he grows.

Most nominally committed men will be focused, at least initially, on only their felt needs—career, money, family, time management, and so on. That's OK. Talk to them about money, and show them what Jesus has to say about it. In other words, give men what they need in the context of what they want.

The BIG Idea

Give men what they need in the context of what they want.

Because our message is based upon the truth of Scripture and the teachings of the Church, we must be relevant while never compromising what is real. Francis Schaeffer said, "Each generation of the church in each setting has the responsibility of communicating the gospel in understandable terms, considering the language and thought-forms of that setting." We must speak God's truth to men in a language they can understand.

For instance, if you are trying to reach men who need Christ, inviting them to a thirty-six-week class on the spirituality of St. Ignatius of Loyola is probably not going to work. On the other hand, you can't expect your men to grow if all you offer is sports events and barbecues.

SOME FINAL GUIDELINES

When you are working with men—at any level of spiritual maturity—a good rule is: Don't trick them! Don't use fun-sounding activities to attract guys, and then get super spiritual with them. This is what cult deprogrammers do, not men who want to reach other men for Christ.

Here are some other guidelines for activities that will attract men who need Christ and men on the fringe:

DO . . .	DON'T . . .
• Have events focused on felt needs: finances, marriage, career, recreation. • Incorporate recreation or hobbies: sports, cars, movies. • Advertise honestly: Yes, it's a Catholic church. Yes, we will talk about God at some point. Yes, we will make it fun and engaging. • Have fun. • Make it easy and natural for men to begin to develop relationships. • Give them the "next step." Invite them back for something else. • Make men want to come back. • Think long term, low pressure.	• Rely solely on events focused on purely spiritual needs: prayer, Bible study, adoration. • Incorporate activities that will make nominal Catholics overly uncomfortable: long-winded prayers, singing multiple hymns in a row, quoting overly pious speakers, or joining hands. • Bait and switch: "Before we play basketball, we have a short thirty-five-minute spiritual film we'd like to show you." • Make men feel guilty. • Ignore the new guy or create contrived exercises to get men to talk. • Make them figure out what they should do next if they are interested. • Drive them away by being too "churchy." • Forget that it takes a long time to make a disciple.

For more specific ideas on activities to reach the different types of men, turn to Appendix C: "Creating Momentum for the Five Types of Men."

Many parishes do a pretty good job of creating momentum. The next chapter will help you make sure these activities move men closer to Christ rather than just become another emotionally satisfying experience. To keep men moving spiritually, one idea makes all the difference: It is absolutely essential that in every instance we capture the momentum we create.

Remember This . . .

- Often the biggest challenge we face is to get guys out of the comfortable patterns they use to stiff-arm God.
- In order for men to choose to be involved in a discipleship activity, we must convince them of the value.
- It can be helpful to think of five types of men: men who need Christ; men who are unengaged Catholics; men who are mature Catholics; men who are leaders; and men who are hurting.
- To provide value, meet men where they are. Different activities appeal to different types of men.
- Personal invitations are the key to getting men to attend. All of your promotional efforts will only make it more likely they will say yes when someone asks them.
- Give men what they need in the context of what they want.

Talk About This . . .

1. When was the last time you did something positive outside of your "comfort zone"? What caused you to take that step? How can this help as you consider how to get new men involved?
2. Think of the last big event you did for men. Which group of men did it focus on? Did the event help you achieve your purpose? How did people find out about the event? Were men personally invited by other men to attend?
3. Think about the men in your parish who are unengaged Catholics. What are some things that might get those men off the spiritual sidelines and into the game?
4. As a team, use the continuum chart on the next page to compile the work you did earlier in the chapter. Write the types of men across the top and the estimated percentages in your parish. Under the line, write down the activities your parish does now—whether or not they are for men only—placing them at the approximate point on the continuum to represent the group(s) of men they reach.
5. Consider the percentage of each type of man in your parish. Are there groups you are "over-targeting"? Are there groups of men in your parish that your current efforts are missing? How could you adjust what you are doing now to help reach all of the men in your parish?

Pray About This . . .

Pray together as a leadership team:

- That men in your parish would realize their need for God and would see your discipleship programs as a way to pursue him.
- For each of the five different types of men in your parish, think of a few men in each category and pray for them by name.
- For God to give you leaders with a heart for men at each stage of their spiritual journey.

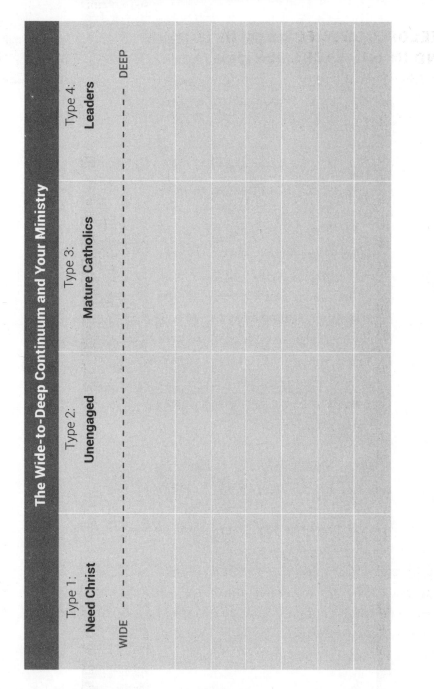

The Wide-to-Deep Continuum and Your Ministry

Type 1: **Need Christ**	Type 2: **Unengaged**	Type 3: **Mature Catholics**	Type 4: **Leaders**
WIDE			DEEP

10
CAPTURE MOMENTUM WITH THE RIGHT NEXT STEP

Many parishes struggle with a roller-coaster men's ministry. An event attracts new men. Four months later, the leadership team is wondering where they all went. This chapter covers the two mistakes that have to do with retaining new men, and gives practical hints on how to move men consistently forward toward authentic discipleship.

HAVE YOU EVER heard a story like this?

> We had an amazing men's retreat last year. This speaker came in and really challenged the guys. He shared how his relationship with his father was pretty bad and how that affected him as an adult. He told about his own failures and how God had reconciled him. He really connected with our men. Guys were getting emotional; groups of men were praying together about their relationships with their own sons and

> wounds from their relationships with their fathers. We had guys recommitting their lives to Christ—it was great.
>
> [Pause . . .] But most of the guys who went are no more involved in our church now than before the event. What happened to all those guys who were praying and crying together? Maybe they were just caught up in the emotion. In fact, I am wondering if some of the guys had authentic experiences at all.

Or perhaps your story is more like this one:

> Five years ago, there was a big men's event in town. We rented a bus, ninety-three guys signed up, and it was awesome! Then three years ago, it was a little bit longer drive and during bad weather, so we only got fifty guys to go. Last year it was local again and we thought we'd get a bunch of guys to go. But we struggled to get twenty-three guys signed up. We ended up going in a few cars, and it just wasn't the same.

Then, the reasons:

- "The priest didn't really support it from the pulpit."
- "It was a bad weekend because of (insert sporting event here)."
- "A lot of guys feel like they've been there, done that."

A ROLLER-COASTER MEN'S MINISTRY

At a meeting of the National Coalition of Men's Ministries, Pastor Sid Woodruff shared a great illustration about riding a roller coaster at a theme park. Living in Central Florida, we know a few things about theme park rides. So we are going to expand on Sid's roller-coaster metaphor.

Imagine climbing in the newest roller coaster with a great sense of anticipation. The shoulder harness comes down and you feel a little shot of adrenaline. You look ahead at the drop that's coming and realize you can't embarrass yourself by climbing out at the last minute like a scared little girl—especially since there are little girls on the roller coaster too, and they don't look all that scared.

You rumble out of the start house, go around the corner, and start up a steep incline. Click, click, click . . . You get about a quarter of the way up, just far enough for all the cars to be suspended vertically, barely clinging to the track, and then you stop. Is it broken? Did someone read the terror on your face and decide to show you mercy?

No!

Over loudspeakers you hadn't noticed before, a countdown begins. At zero, you are catapulted up toward the sky. As you approach the top of the hill, you quickly ask God to take care of your children and wife and then try to decide if you want to die with your eyes open or shut.

The bottom drops out; or rather, you are snatched back down again. The laws of physics have been overcome! The roller coaster didn't leave the tracks! Now, the ride really begins. You are yanked around hairpin corners, shot up inclines, dropped down into metallic ravines, and flipped upside down a few times for good measure.

What was terrifying soon turns into fun. The sights of the theme park shooting by, the sound of the others on the ride yelling and screaming with delight, your own joy as you realize, "I'm not going to die." A few more bone wrenching corners, and then it calms, followed by an upside-down twisting, turning flip inspired by the double helix structure of DNA. You hear yourself shouting with glee, "Is that all you've got? You can do better than that!" And then you come around the corner and . . . you stop.

You're back in the little starting house again. The ride operators are looking at you with the same disinterested stares they had when you left. There's another mass of expectant park guests waiting to take your seat on the ride. As you stand up and climb out, you look back and realize I'm getting off the ride exactly where I got on. I really haven't gone anywhere.

This story contains many parallels to men's ministry. The big event, the retreat, the small groups have been executed. Done correctly, these events can catapult your ministry forward. But, too often, several months or even a year or two later, leaders look around and realize their ministries are right back where they started. Instead of having a men's ministry that grows, albeit through peaks and valleys, their men's ministry stagnates. They are not able to capture and sustain the momentum. They have a roller-coaster men's ministry.

If you were to make a chart of this kind of men's ministry, it might look something like this:

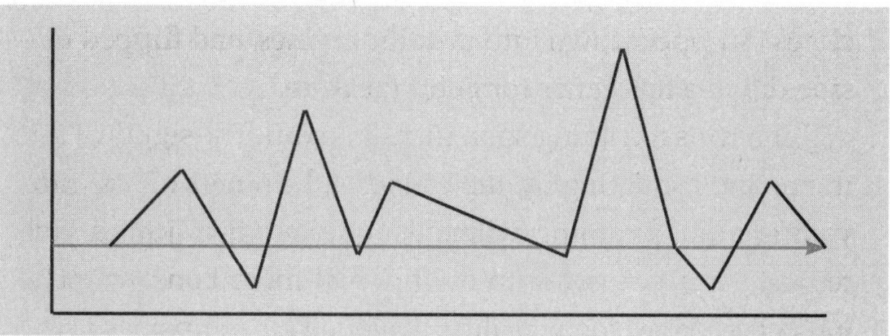

FIGURE 9

Typical Roller-Coaster Men's Ministry

What about your ministry to men? Are you so frustrated that you're ready to shout, "Stop this ride! I want to get off!" Can you identify more with the valleys than with the peaks? Does your men's ministry feel like a series of highs—great men's events, experiences, revivals—while there is no real difference today in the spiritual commitment of your men? Have you seen a substantial increase in the number of men who are actively pursuing discipleship from a year ago or five years ago? If you don't like your answers, you can get off the roller coaster and start taking your men toward a new destination.

TWO TRAPS IN MEN'S MINISTRY

But before you can get off the roller coaster, you have to know how you got on in the first place. If a roller-coaster men's ministry is the problem, what is the cause? In our experience, there are two different traps that men's ministries fall into.

Trap #1: The Personality-Driven Men's Ministry

Some churches have men's ministries that go extremely well for a couple of years and then run out of steam. They have several great events each year, ongoing small groups for men, big groups going to men's conferences, well attended mission trips . . . you get the picture.

But then, over the course of several months, it all just seems to die out. The next men's retreat comes around and it's not very well-organized. Only half the number of guys who came last year show up. Small groups are disappearing, and the guy in charge of them seems to have lost interest. Generally, activities just sort of fade away.

This is the classic symptom of a personality-driven men's ministry. In this scenario a dynamic, spiritually mature leader gathers a group of men around him and organizes the men's ministry. He has the respect of his pastor and the leadership of the parish, and they give him the resources he needs to make things happen. His organizational skills help ensure high quality events that guys appreciate.

Unfortunately, one day this leader gets a promotion that requires additional travel. And his right-hand man has to reduce his involvement when his mother faces a health crisis and has to move in with him. They haven't recruited any additional leaders, so there's no one else ready or willing to step up. It's like someone taking their foot off the gas as the car speeds down the road. It keeps going for a while on sheer momentum. But soon it will coast to a stop.

Trap #2: The Event-Driven Man's Ministry

Perhaps your men's ministry goes through a series of ups and downs several times throughout each year: You spent a couple months hyping the big men's rally and barbecue right after Labor Day. The men of your parish get pumped up. They sign up for the event several weeks in advance. Everyone is talking about last year when they roasted a whole pig on a spit. That's gross and fascinating at the same time. The event comes and you have a great turnout. Everyone is excited about getting your new parish year started right for the men.

And then . . . well, I guess we'd better start getting ready for the Super Bowl party in February. Then . . . the spring men's weekend. Then . . . the men's conference again.

For this parish, men's ministry is a series of "blips." Each year, there are three or four events that get guys excited. But in between, it's still a struggle to get men to work in the various parish programs, and the monthly pancake breakfast is just about the only other men's activity available.

This is an event-driven men's ministry. Of course, events for men are important. We need lots of entry points for men to become involved in the life of the parish and to get exposed to the gospel and the sacraments. But if the event is all there is, eventually men will stop coming.

Often the ministries and programs of our parishes are like skyscrapers in New York City. Each of them exists without clear connection to other parish programs.

You can escape the personality-driven men's ministry trap by continually recruiting and empowering leadership, which we covered in detail in chapter seven. Feel free to glance there now to review the strategies and suggestions for renewing your leadership.

How do you escape an event-driven men's ministry? Have a strategy in place to capture the momentum your events create, and channel it into the right next step for every man.

Would you turn on the air conditioning in your house in the middle of the summer and then leave the doors and windows open? Of course not! In the same way, it takes a tremendous amount of work and energy to overcome inertia in the men by creating value and momentum. Doesn't it make sense to have a concrete plan to capture that momentum and keep men moving forward in their relationship with God?

OVERCOMING A SKYSCRAPER MINISTRY

Imagine you are visiting New York City and a friend takes you to the top of a skyscraper. As you look over the beautiful city, he points to a building across the street and tells you about the wonderful restaurant on the top floor. "Why don't we just jump over there right now and have some lunch?" You'd look across at the building, then down at the street and conclude that your friend was crazy. It's ridiculous to think you could jump forty-five feet to another skyscraper.

Often the ministries and programs of our parishes are like skyscrapers in New York City. Each of them exists without clear connection to other parish programs. A person is involved in religious education, the liturgy committee, and a short-term mission trip, but there are no real connections between the initiatives. So getting a man who attends Mass to join a couples' small group or a men's Bible study is like asking him to jump from one skyscraper to another. The ironic thing is this: Some people are willing to make the jump. There are always the committed few who will take a leap of faith and dive headfirst into a new opportunity. In fact, enough people make these jumps in most parishes to prevent us from seeing how poorly we have integrated a believable process of discipleship. But the vast majority of people will stay exactly where they are unless we build bridges to connect the opportunities together and make it obvious how to move from one step to the next. That's what it means to capture momentum.

TWO COMMON MISTAKES AFTER CREATING MOMENTUM

There are two common mistakes that we tend to make after creating a value with a man: We do too little, or we attempt to do too much.

First, we do too little. How many times have you seen a ministry expend all its energy planning "the big event," only to pack up and go home after the closing "amen"? This is the classic event-driven men's ministry.

We hold a men's retreat or seminar; the man has a "blip." Next year we invite him . . . another "blip." The year after? "Blip" again. After a few years, we have a lot of "blip" men, but there is no ongoing spiritual development.

If we are not careful, men will think this is what it means to be a good Catholic. Or, they will lose interest because they don't see any lasting impact in their own lives. A roller-coaster men's ministry builds a resistance for men getting involved. Because they know, deep in their hearts, it's not really going to lead anywhere; your men (and your pastor) will become inoculated against a viable discipleship process.

Second, attempting too much can be just as fruitless. For instance, you invite men to a big Super Bowl barbecue with lots of red meat and a giant screen TV. You encourage them to bring neighbors and friends, and several men who rarely darken the parish doors come. Then at halftime you get up and offer them an opportunity to join a forty-week study of the book of Revelation in the original Greek. A little over the top, but you get the point. So how do you walk the line between these two extremes? Always have a right next step.

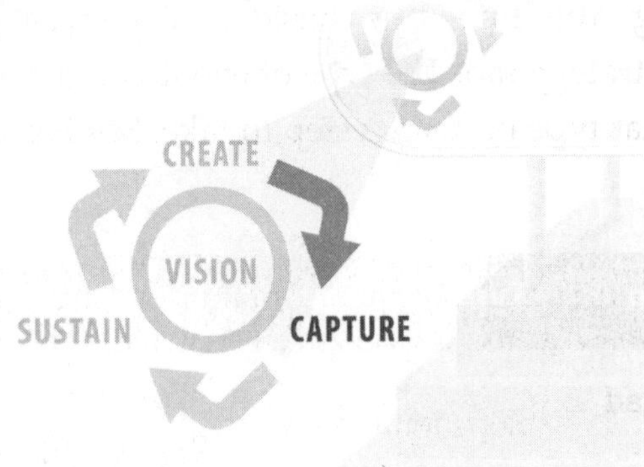

GIVE MEN A RIGHT NEXT STEP

When you plan an event or activity for men, make the follow-up opportunities part of your event planning. In other words, don't create momentum without a plan for how you will capture it (ever!). We'll cover each of the keys to successfully capturing momentum in detail, but for now here is the list:

- Make the follow-up fit the event.
- Right-size the commitment you are asking for.
- Always have an ending point.
- Choose good "second gear" material.
- Start new groups for new men.
- Help men take the next step—on the spot.

Make the Follow-Up Fit the Event

As you plan an event, determine the types of men you will be targeting. You'll need to consider this as you plan the follow-up strategy too. The type of event you have will determine what type of *capture* step to take. See Figure 10 for some ideas.

Type of Men	Type of Event	Follow-Up Ideas
Men Who Need Christ	Super Bowl party	Softball team sign-up; adventure trip; new introductory small groups
Unengaged Catholics	Reroof a widow's house	Information meeting for mission trip; formation of servant ministry teams
Mature Catholics	Men's seminar or retreat	Small groups; class; service opportunity
Leaders of Catholics	Lunch to discuss vision	Pray for men; attend a leaders' meeting as a guest

FIGURE 10

Right-Size the Commitment You Are Asking for

Don't ask men to overreach based on event enthusiasm. A man may initially be excited about the intense forty-week Bible study on godly manhood. But on Monday his customers start complaining, on Tuesday he remembers he's fifteen days late with his mortgage payment, and by Wednesday his enthusiasm has waned considerably.

You've driven a car and accidentally shifted from first to fourth gear. What happens? It's the same when we ask men to do too much too soon. They get bogged down. Most men on the fringe don't want to do a lot of preparation. Many men are not going to read a two-hundred-page book. So the event follow-up needs to scream to the man, "You can do this!" It must be something he can actually visualize himself doing with excitement. It has to be a "second gear" idea.

Always Have an Ending Point

We also can ask men to do too much by requiring open-ended commitments. Consider a man who has an experience that inspires him to seek a closer walk with God. He joins a weekly men's Bible study. Soon, either because his life circumstances change or perhaps because of overcommitment, his participation in the group starts to suffer. He misses a week here and there, then two weeks in a row, then three weeks. Finally, he just stops coming altogether. He leaves the group quietly, almost slinking away, feeling guilty that he let the group down, because there was no graceful exit strategy.

Now imagine that same man making a six-week commitment to meet with a group of men. If the circumstances change, he knows that he will only have to "tough it out" for a few more weeks to finish what he started. He leaves the group not in failure but with a sense of fulfillment and accomplishment. Which man will be more likely to join a small group at the next opportunity?

To reinforce this concept, you can even celebrate at the end of each cycle. This could be your time to share stories about how God has worked in your lives over the past six weeks, as well as say a formal good-bye to a man whose other commitments will not allow him to continue. Your group might even "commission" him for his new undertaking, making him feel like he is being sent by the group to the next thing, instead of feeling like he has abandoned them.

Choose Good "Second Gear" Material

Look for "cookies on the bottom shelf" materials that raise significant issues and deal with them in the context of our Catholic faith. Men will make a one-time, short-term commitment to something that seems "doable."

The case study in the box below illustrates two other common mistakes we often make. Can you find them?

Mistakes in Men's Ministry: A Case Study

One parish we'll call "St. Rockie's" shared that they seem to have reached a "ceiling" of sorts with the number of men who would engage in their small groups. When they were asked what they were doing to recruit men, their strategy seemed pretty sound, at first. They would have men's events in the parish that had a broad appeal to men. Every event was extremely well-attended. At each event, they would offer an opportunity to join in a group for ongoing study. They were using good, second-gear material. They were only asking for a short-term commitment. Everything else seemed fine.

Then they were asked the question: How are you signing guys up for the small groups? "Simple," they said. "We list all the groups on a separate piece of paper in the back. Each group lists the name of the leader, when and where they are meeting, and how many spots they have available. So they find a group that's convenient and write down their name, and then the leader follows up. But only a few new guys ever sign up. And even those that do often don't show up."

Start New Groups for New Men

The first error "St. Rockie's" made was listing groups with the number of spots available. A man who looks at that quickly realizes he is walking into an established group. Who else is in the group? How long have they been meeting? He is obviously going to be the "new guy." If you ever switched schools growing up, you remember what lunch was like for the first week. Everybody already had "their" table. You didn't really know how open they might be to a new kid sitting with them.

We might all be adults now, but that fear of rejection never goes away. Always start new groups for your follow-up.

Help Men Take the Step . . . on the Spot

Did you spot the second error? Don't have guys write their names on the list and tell them "you'll get back to them." You want men to leave feeling like they've already made the commitment. So whatever your next step, always ask for an on-site commitment.

Here's a proven method to get two thirds of your men into follow-up small groups:

Hold an event that reaches a specific target group of men, like a seminar. Promote the event with—say it with us now—personal invitations. Before the event, recruit leaders who will commit to running a six-week follow-up group and have about one leader for every eight or nine men you expect to attend the seminar. (If two-thirds of the men sign up, that will give you groups of five or six for each leader.)

At the beginning or middle of the event, announce that there is a "next step" for everyone after the event. Show them the material they will be using, and make sure they understand that it is a short-term commitment. This gives them time to absorb the idea.

The following examples can be used to explain the benefit of the follow-up groups:

> "If you give me $100 now, I'll give you $200 at the end of the seminar. How many of you would take me up on that offer?" Every hand usually goes up.

> "Now, let me offer you a different deal. If you will give me $200 now, I will give you $1000 in six weeks. Double the investment of the first deal, but five times the return. How many of you would take that deal?" Usually someone stands up and jokingly starts to take out his wallet at this point.

> "Well, guys, this is exactly the deal I'm offering you. If you will give me about eight hours of time over the next day at this event, I'm going to give you a pretty good return on your investment. But if you will double that investment, and spend another eight hours over the next six weeks meeting with some other guys from this group to go over this study guide we are giving you, you will get five times as much out of it as if you just listened to me alone."
>
> "The fact is that I can only give you information that will make you think during the seminar. If you really want to see how this will apply to your life, spend some time unpacking these issues with a few other guys who live in your world."

Provide several sessions for small-group discussion throughout the event. This helps model the follow-up groups and gets men talking to each other. We often hear of parishes that had to break up the discussions to move to the next session.

About three quarters of the way through the event, instead of going into another small group discussion time, let your men know you will now be forming the groups for follow-up. Have each leader stand, introduce himself, and share when and where his group will be meeting. "Hi, I'm Don Smith, and my group is going to meet at the Denny's on the corner of Fifth and Main on Thursday mornings at 6:30 A.M." And so on.

After all the leaders of groups introduce themselves, tell the men that for the next discussion time you would like them to pick a group that they might be interested in continuing with after the event. Remind them it's only a six-week commitment. Tell them that even if they don't plan on attending a group afterward, just to go ahead and pick one of the discussion times.

At this point, all the men in the room are staring at you, and you have to say, "OK, right now! Pick someone to sit with! Get going! They will finally start moving, and before you know it each man will be sitting in a circle with some other men. It's messy, and it looks unorganized, but it absolutely works! We guarantee it! The secret to this is that men are smart and will figure it out. You don't have to micromanage the process. In fact, micromanaging will actually reduce your effectiveness.

Before they get into the discussion, the leaders pass around a sheet of paper to collect each man's name, phone, and email. Then they confirm the time and location of their first meeting—make it within the next seven days—and adjust it if necessary to meet the men's needs. Then they briefly look at the material they will be using. (We provide a simple sixteen-page "Life Plan" with Man in the Mirror events.) If they have time, they'll go into the discussion questions for the session that just ended.

Even a man who might have gone reluctantly to sit in a group will become somewhat invested in when and where they will meet, what they will talk about, and who will be there.

Does it work? At events where parishes use this method just the way it's described, over two thirds of the men indicate that they have decided to join the follow-up groups.

Perhaps even more excitingly, the percentage of men who have never been in a small group before and choose to be in the follow-up groups is even higher.

THE "NEXT STEP" MIND-SET

You can get everything else right, but if you consistently fail to capture momentum you have created, you will not build a sustainable ministry.

> In every interaction you have with a man, whether it is one-on-one over lunch, a small group kickoff, a men's retreat or seminar, or any other activity, you should always be thinking, "What is a reasonable next step?" and then constantly communicating these steps to men.

Every leader in your ministry needs to have a capture momentum, "next step" mind-set. Always show men a right next step. Getting men to take the first step and then not showing them what's next is like leading a man to Christ and then abandoning him to live in the world with no discipleship. If you are not going to follow up, perhaps it would be better for Christ's kingdom to not raise men's expectations in the first place.

Will capturing momentum eliminate peaks and valleys in your ministry to men? No. You will still have men come and go. You'll still have events or activities that draw lots of men who drop off. But over time your trend line will be sloping upward, indicating a sustainable ministry that continues to produce passionate disciples. (See Figure 11.)

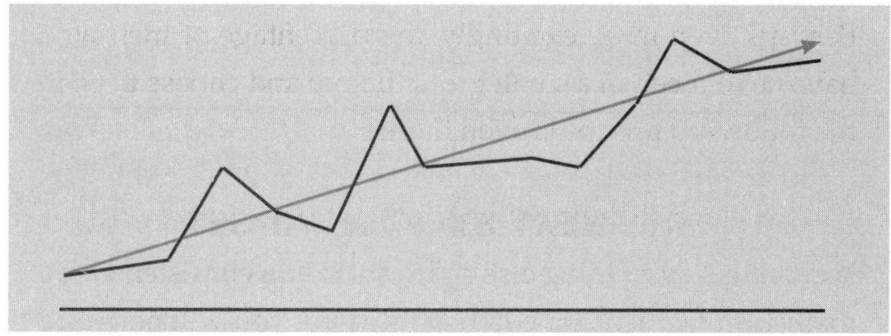

FIGURE 11
A Sustainable Men's Ministry
(General Upward Trend in Discipling Men)

One of the primary missions of the space shuttle is to put a satellite into space. The shuttle blasts into orbit, then an astronaut uses a robotic arm to pick up the satellite and place it in space, where it takes on the speed and trajectory of the shuttle itself. All is according to plan.

Remember Skylab? (All you under-forty-year-olds, check it out online.) The Skylab was a large satellite work-station—a precursor to the International Space Station. The United States put it into orbit in 1973, with plans of going up in the space shuttle in 1979 to boost it into a higher orbit. Unfortunately, the space shuttle wasn't ready until 1981. Skylab didn't have enough momentum to hold its orbit that long, and it crashed to earth in late 1979. Luckily, the only casualty was an Australian cow.

> **The BIG Idea**
>
> Whenever you create momentum, always show men a right next step.

Be careful not to leave men in your parish hanging. If you use an event to blast a man into a spiritual experience that draws him closer to God, don't just hope he can maintain his orbit. When a man crashes to the ground, there is always a lot more to worry about than the life of an Australian cow.

So far, we have discussed how to build your ministry around a vision, highlighted how to create momentum with men, and now how to capture that momentum. In the next chapter we will discuss how to sustain change in the men who have entered your discipleship process. We are only one step away from chapter twelve, which will help you build a concrete plan to reach the men in your parish.

Remember This . . .

- Avoid a personality-driven men's ministry by constantly recruiting and renewing your leadership (see chapter seven).
- Escape an event-driven ministry by capturing the momentum that your events create.
- Don't make men "leap" from one opportunity to the next. Build bridges that make it easy and intuitive for a man to move forward in his spiritual journey.
- Always give men a right next step.
- Remember these hints for your next strategy:
    - Make the follow-up fit the event.
    - Right-size the commitment you are asking for.
    - Always have an ending point.
    - Choose good "second gear" material.
    - Start new groups for new men.
    - Help men take the next step on the spot.

Talk About This . . .

1. Do you feel like you have been on a roller coaster in your own spiritual journey? What seems to cause the peaks and valleys?
2. Does the roller coaster describe your men's ministry? If so, do you feel like you've fallen into the trap of an event-driven ministry? Personality-driven ministry? Both? What effect has this had on your energy and commitment to forming men as disciples in your parish?
3. List the events or activities you have done for men in your parish over the last few months. Has there been a *capture* strategy in place for these events? If not, what could you have done to capture the momentum you created? If so, how could you have improved it?
4. What is the next event you have planned for men? Brainstorm with your team about how you will capture the momentum of this activity.

Pray About This . . .

Pray together as a leadership team:

- That God will give the men in your parish a renewed desire to know him.
- That your ministry will always provide a clear path for men to take from one opportunity to the next.
- That God continues to bond your leadership team together as a band of brothers, focused on fulfilling the Great Commission among men.

11
SUSTAIN MOMENTUM THROUGH RELATIONSHIPS

From the event, to the next step, to . . . what? Once you get your men and your men's ministry off the roller coaster, how do you sustain spiritual progress? If you don't do anything, spiritual excitement will turn into little more than good intentions. One thing's for sure: Men won't make it on their own. But together, they can become authentic disciples who can change the world.

TO SUSTAIN MOMENTUM with men, get them into real relationships with other men who are seeking Christ. You can't sustain momentum without small groups and one-on-one relationships.

Why is this so important? First, you want to help men maintain the spiritual progress they have made. This is particularly important for men early in their spiritual journey—those who need Christ, as well as cultural Catholics. Second, you want to get men into regular contact with God through his Word and through the sacraments. This is a particular focus for men who are mature Catholics and leaders, and those who want to be. Building relationships will help you meet both of these objectives.

KEEPING CAPTURED GROUND

Military history is filled with stories about soldiers who gripe about surrendering the ground they shed their blood to gain. "Take that hill!" they are told. "It is an integral part of our strategy!" And they do it, fighting valiantly to defeat the enemy and capture the ground—only to abandon it when the strategic winds shift in the command center. Pretty soon the soldier loses confidence that there is any strategy at all. The cost is too high, and the reward is too fleeting.

Every effort you make that draws a man forward in his spiritual journey has a cost of its own: the time, energy, and focus of the leaders who planned and participated; and the opportunity the man loses participating in this activity instead of some other priority in his life. If you work hard to gain ground in the battle for men's time and attention but then don't find ways to sustain that effort, you'll just find yourself starting over, and the men themselves will begin to lose heart, feeling that nothing ever changes. As leaders, we must apply consistent effort, since progress in a man's spiritual journey is usually measured in small steps over a long period of time.

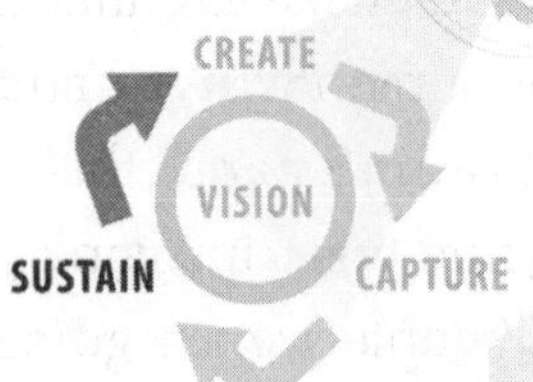

A LONG-TERM PERSPECTIVE

A ministry to men has to be more than just events; it must be about helping men to become mature in Christ. Again, it takes a long time to make a disciple. Almost always, discipleship takes place over a period of years and in the context of significant relationships with other men.

Taking a "long-term, low-pressure" approach is important. There is no such thing as a systematic, rapid spiritual growth. We must give men permission to stand around the rim of what we are doing and observe. Give them permission to buy in at their own pace, and let them come on board at their own level of involvement.

If you want to help other men grow in Christ, you will often feel that you want men to be successful more than they want it themselves. It would be easy for us to become impatient with new men who were not as mature as we might wish. Don't make men feel guilty because they are not becoming as "spiritual" as you want them to be.

This is one of the biggest problems we see in men's ministry leaders. The leaders are frustrated, angry, and even bitter with their men because they are not as committed as the leaders would like. For example, a trainer was supposed to be a speaker at a retreat one time when the leader of the men's mission trip stood up to make an announcement. "The mission trip is less than a month away and we only have four men signed up. I know in a parish this large there are a lot of men who could go on this trip. Don't you know how fortunate you are? The people we are going to serve don't have anything. Frankly, I wonder whether some of you ought to seriously consider the level of your commitment to Christ."

After a few more minutes of his aggressive talk, the trainer felt like standing up in the back and saying, "Look, I'll go on the mission trip—as long as you stay home. As angry as you are, I don't want to go anywhere for a week with you." Men can sense anger and frustration, and they won't want any part of it. Our job is not to produce results—it's simply to be faithful. As St. Teresa of Calcutta said, "God does not call you to be successful; he calls you to be faithful."

SHOW MEN CHRIST VERSUS FIX THEIR BEHAVIOR

Too often we ask men to conform to our Christian men's subculture as a show of spirituality. "Use these buzz words. Pray with this posture." When this happens, we can end up asking men to fit into a way of behaving or acting at the expense of inviting him to a deeper experience of his faith life. Or, we ask them to perform certain activities to show their commitment to God. "If you love God, you will be in church on Wednesday night." One man readily responds to calls for "performance" Catholicism

Q & A

What do you do when guys just don't "get it"?

You've been working to show Christ to a guy for months. But it seems like he goes out of his way to smoke and use foul language whenever your Christian friends come around. You know what? He's waiting to see if you'll be judgmental. Instead, love him. Get your friends in on the act. Surround him with godly men and he'll eventually decide he wants what you've got.

because that's the nature of his relationship with his own dad, who always made love conditional based upon his son's performance. It's ironic. The more we try to influence "behavior," the less real lasting change in behavior we see. Such an approach will simply burden men and wear them out.

When men come to a prayer breakfast, conference, Bible study, or Mass, they come because they have an unmet need—a "void" to be filled. They come looking for a piece of bread they can take away that will nourish their souls; they come thirsty for living water.

Rather than show men a list of "dos" and "don'ts," we must show them Christ. Our job is not to "fix" their behavior, but rather to make Christ ever more attractive so that he can do his life-transforming work on them. God's grace changes men—not without some effort on their part, but when we help men connect with Jesus, he works the change in behavior from the inside out. He changes the desires of the man. We can only give a man a new rulebook; Jesus will give him a new heart.

MEN WHO NEED CHRIST

Nowhere is a flawed central focus for forming men as disciples more damaging than with men who need Christ. A man who has built up regular participation in one of your more accessible activities—like basketball or the softball team—is easily pushed away by someone telling him he's not behaving "correctly."

It is sometimes difficult for leaders to understand how to apply and sustain steps to engaging men early in their spiritual journey. After all, you can't really expect a man whose only experience with your parish is participating in the sports outreach ministry to sign up for a twenty-four-week small group.

Sustaining change in a man who is just becoming aware of his need for Christ is much more about keeping "captured ground" than leapfrogging him to daily devotions and to an accountability group.

For men at this stage, sustaining momentum may take place with opportunities very similar to the *create* step that got him involved in the first place. Remember, the key is relationships.

Consider the softball team activity as an example. One of your leaders, "Sam," has a neighbor named "Pete." After trading several favors, loaning each other tools and watching a playoff game together, Sam mentions he's on a parish softball team. When Pete expresses interest, Sam invites him.

The season goes great. Everyone has lots of fun on the team. No one takes it too seriously, though they all enjoy winning. Pete gets to know a few guys on the team. At the end of the season, they have a barbecue to celebrate, and the pastor comes to thank the guys for planning and representing the parish with good sportsmanship. The *create* step was the invitation to join the softball team. The *capture* step was the barbecue at the end of the year. Now what? First, has Pete really progressed in his spiritual journey? Certainly! For ten weeks running he has spent an evening with a group of mostly Catholic guys. They say a quick prayer before and after the game. Pete has begun to see that these guys are "normal." And there are some men who have earned his respect.

Now you must find a way for Pete to maintain the relationships that he has begun to build. It may be another season of softball, or a weekly businessmen's luncheon that some of the guys attend. As relationships begin to grow, Pete will have more opportunities to see Christ in these men's lives.

SUSTAIN CHANGE BY CREATING A CULTURE OF PRAYER

One day, Bill, whose wife had just died of cancer, was talking with one of original authors, Pat, whose friend, Tom Skinner, was sick with leukemia. Pat said, "He's very sick. I guess the only thing we can do is pray." Bill looked into Pat's face and said, "No, the thing we can do is pray." We can't do anything without God's blessing, but we can do all things when we tap into his designated way of releasing his will in men's lives—prayer. Prayer is the currency of our personal relationship with Jesus. It will do us no good to leave it in one account. We must take some out and spend it on men's souls. Prayer is the thing we can do.

Ensure that prayer is a part of everything you do for the men of your parish. Train your leaders to integrate prayer into every activity. No man participating in an activity related to the parish is going to be surprised by the inclusion of a prayer during an event. Your leadership team ought also to be built on a foundation of prayer. But don't merely ask God to become a part of what you want to do in your parish and city. Instead, pray that you will become part of what God wants to do in your parish and community.

HELP MEN DEVELOP A LOVE FOR GOD IN HIS WORD AND IN THE SACRAMENTS

Disciples are "pupils." They are students of Jesus. They are men who desire to become more like Christ. But to become like him, they must first know him.

> We can say with confidence that we have never known a man whose life was changed in any significant way apart from regular reading and prayer with God's Word.

Some groups study Catholic books, but this is no substitute for bringing men into direct contact with his living Word. All men are affected by God's Word when they are exposed to it regularly. Have you noticed that when you consistently read the Bible, you begin to understand it better? Your desire for the Scriptures grows the more you interact with them. Unfortunately, the opposite is also true. When a man doesn't read the Scriptures very often, his desire for them doesn't have a chance to grow.

Hand-in-hand with God's Word in enabling men to know and love Jesus are the sacraments. The Catechism tells us that the sacraments "strengthen faith and express it," and are a means "by which divine life is dispensed to us" (*CCC*, 1133, 1131). Men should be welcomed and encouraged to attend Mass weekly, to receive the Eucharist in a state of grace, and to receive the sacrament of confession regularly as a powerful aid in battling sin. Additionally, many parishes offer Eucharistic adoration, in which taking time apart to simply be with Jesus and adore his real presence in the Eucharist can be a particularly powerful opportunity for a man's personal relationship with Christ to develop. Together with the Word of God, the sacraments are a mode of Christ's presence to us, and they are indispensable in helping a man sustain the spiritual progress he has begun.

DEVELOPING DISCIPLE-MAKERS TO SUSTAIN YOUR MINISTRY

In his book, *The Lost Art of Disciple Making*, Leroy Eims tells the story of a missionary named John, who spent the bulk of his years of service meeting with a few young men. Abruptly, his work was cut short when all missionaries were suddenly asked to leave the country.

An observer who had once viewed John's ministry with skepticism years later marveled, "I look at what has come out of John's life. One of the men he worked with is now a professor who mightily uses God to reach and train scores of university students. Another is leading a discipling team of about fourteen men and women. And yet another is in a nearby city with a group of thirty-five growing disciples. Three others have gone to other countries as missionaries. God is blessing their work."

Keep your eye out for men who want to make disciples. Obviously you need to be involved with men at all levels. But can there be any doubt? The greatest return on your time will come from investing in a few "FAT" men—those who are faithful, available, and teachable (see 2 Timothy 2:2).

The focus of a men's ministry leader should be to make disciples of men who will in turn disciple others, and so on. This was the method of Jesus. Your ministry to men will grow in proportion to your ability to build not just disciples but disciple-makers.

RECRUIT SHEPHERDS, NOT TEACHERS

Possibly the most important aspect of sustaining momentum is to make sure each of your men really feels like somebody cares about him. Look for knowledgeable leaders who are eager to show men the love of Christ.

Clark Cothran, a senior pastor of a Protestant church, draws the distinction between two types of small-group leaders: one is a "question asker," the other is an "answer giver." One is a "group guide," the other is a "know-it-all narrator." One is a "dialogue traffic cop," the other is a "doctrine cop." Men will respond best to leaders who help them find the correct answers to their questions without giving them the answer. Men who guide men without showing off their knowledge, and help facilitate lively discussions, rather than showing up a man whose theological knowledge is still developing.

At a church of five thousand parishioners in California, Wes Brown, the men's minister (yes, full time), experienced a quantum leap in effectiveness when he changed his leadership model from "teaching" to "shepherding." In the beginning, he recruited "teachers" to lead his small groups. Success was modest. After eleven years, he had 137 men in small groups. Then he realized that what men really needed was someone who cared about them personally. He changed to a "shepherding" model, and his ministry exploded to include 750 men in just four years—a 550 percent increase!

LOVE YOUR WEAK MEN, DISCIPLE YOUR STRONG

Zechariah explains the role of a good shepherd further:

> Then the LORD said to me, "Take once more the implements of a worthless shepherd. For lo, I am raising up in the land a shepherd who does not care for the perishing, or seek the wandering, or heal the maimed, or nourish the sound, but devours the flesh of the fat ones, tearing off even their hooves." (Zechariah 11:15–16)

We can define the fourfold role of a good shepherd by looking at the opposite role of the worthless shepherd in this passage:

- He cares for the sheep that are young.
- He cares for the injured.
- He cares for those threatened by death.
- He feeds the hungry.

This passage illustrates a basic rule for discipleship: *Love your weak men, and disciple your strong*. A good shepherd goes after those who are threatened by death. This might be men who don't know Christ, or men who are on their way to making major mistakes in their life. He creates a safe place where men with broken wings can heal—men injured by financial crisis, divorce, grief, addictions, or emotional issues. He takes care of the young, spiritually and physically.

There will always be some men who consistently drain your emotional and spiritual energy. Good shepherds are committed to loving their weak men.

At the same time, God wants you to invest in faithful men who can disciple others. The faithful shepherd makes sure he feeds the healthy. How do you know when you should stop making an investment in a man who doesn't seem to be making progress? It has to be a matter of prayerful consideration between you and God. Don't give up on any man—always be friendly, interested, and available. However, there may come a time when God wants you to invest your time and energy in other men.

There are two errors leaders can make: to kick a man out of the nest too soon, and to not challenge men to get out of the nest when it's time. "Disciple the strong" means men need to grow. If you don't help them, they will go to another church. We've all heard it said or said it ourselves: "I just didn't feel like I was being fed there." A good shepherd will feed the healthy.

In addition to feeding the healthy, a good shepherd propels strong men to take their next steps. He doesn't let men become complacent in their spiritual progress. Instead, he challenges them to step up to new opportunities, encourages them to go deeper in their faith, and urges them to serve others.

A PERSONAL INVESTMENT IN EVERY MAN

Your parish already has many activities that men can be involved in. It doesn't have to be a "men's-only" activity to help men grow spiritually. Remember the five groups of men in your parish and community?

If you want to sustain momentum with each type of man, someone has to get to know each man in your parish well enough to know where he is on his spiritual pilgrimage and what he needs to do to take the next step.

You have to develop enough leaders to take a personal interest in every man. Then you need to have ministry opportunities that will help men from each category move forward. This is where the hard work comes—there are no shortcuts here.

Men are good at keeping each other at a comfortable distance. It takes consistent time together to develop beyond the level of mere acquaintances. We described these in detail earlier in this book, but here is a partial list of ways to engage men in relationships:

- Bible studies
- Ongoing ministry projects, such as mentoring teenagers
- Issue-oriented men's curricula (family, marriage, work, etc.)
- Spiritual direction
- Early morning leadership development with the pastor
- Prayer groups
- Issue-oriented support groups—divorce recovery, dealing with grief, etc.

Obviously, overlap will occur. Bible studies will encourage prayer. Book studies will address biblical themes. Accountability groups will study books. The key is to engage men in ways that relate to where they live, work, and play.

Create a variety of opportunities for men to get better acquainted with Christ, since men will be motivated to know him in many different ways. A restaurant with only one item on the menu will soon go out of business. The greater variety you offer, the more a man will find something that engages him where he walks.

SUSTAIN BY REACHING MEN'S HEADS, HEARTS, AND HANDS

In chapter three, we introduced you to the concept that the truth must be understood, believed, and lived out using the keywords head, heart, and hands. This is an excellent paradigm to help you determine the "content" of your discipleship program. In other words, look at what you want men to know, believe, and do, and determine where in your parish a man has the opportunity to learn, build his faith, and put it all into practice.

One church in Orlando used this paradigm to create a chart (see Figure 12, "What Does a Disciple Look Like?"). Here's the key question: If you were only to have a man for five years, what would be the things you would want him to know, believe, and do in relation to for major areas of relationship—God, his family, the church, and the world—to feel like you had effectively discipled him?

For instance, you would want a man to know God's attributes and character, to believe that God loves him and died for him, and know how to draw close to him in his Word and in the sacraments. See the chart (Figure 12) for suggestions in all four relational spheres.

What Does a Disciple Look Like?
If you knew that you were only going to have a man for five years, what are the ideas and experiences that you would want him to get to consider yourself a "success"?

ASPECT:	RELATIONAL SPHERE			
	GOD	FAMILY	PARISH	WORLD
HEAD (What do you know?)	Theology The Catechism Scripture	Roles of hus-bands/fathers Family as convenant/ significance in God's plan	Vision, mis-sion, values Spiritual gifts Ecclesiology	Missions Worldview
HANDS (What do you do?)	Worship Spiritual disciplines	Communica-tion Discipline Leadership Sacrifice	Ministry Stewardship Leadership Accountability	Vocations Missions Evangelization Social justice Community
HEART (What do you love?)	Love God above self and have no idols	Love family before self	Love church/ parish family before self	Love those who are des-perate without Christ Love those who are suffering devastation from sin

Based on a chart developed by the leadership of University Presbyterian Church in Orlando, Florida.

FIGURE 12

You can take this chart and adapt it for your parish's discipleship goals. Use it to audit your activities and events for men. But next to each item, ask what your parish currently does well for men. This will help you identify potential holes or gaps where your (men's-only) initiatives could have a bigger impact. Then you can plan to tackle areas that are not being addressed by other ministries of the parish. A blank version is included at the end of the chapter to allow you to customize the chart for your parish.

THE ARROWS ARE IMPORTANT TOO!

Sustaining momentum is the third "gear" in the engine that runs your conveyor belt. It is often the least exciting of the three-part *Create-Capture-Sustain* strategy. And yet it is here that the majority of spiritual growth takes place, and it is how you can best make sure no man is left behind.

Be sure to communicate to the leaders of your *capture* steps that their job is to help men make a seamless transition to *sustain* activities. It's not enough to point men in the right direction and say, "Good luck!" We must have the mind-set that it is our responsibility to take men to the next step. Two previous examples of this are personal invitations (chapter nine) and getting an on-site commitment (chapter ten).

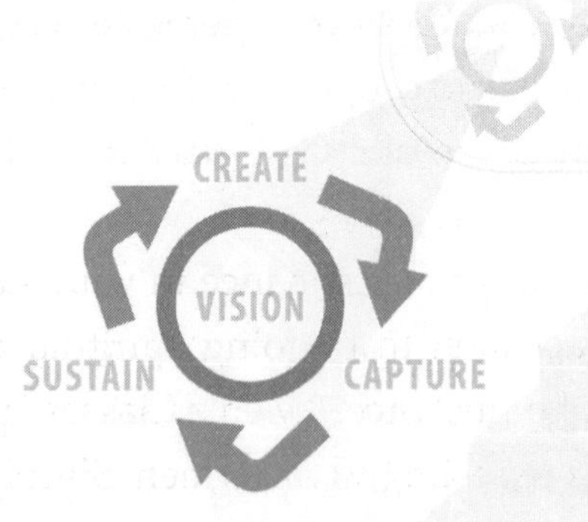

In the third and fourth week of the follow-up, the leaders begin introducing the idea of the men coming with their wives to the class on Sunday.

At their last meeting, the leader might say something like this, "Guys, this has been a lot of fun. As I mentioned before, our next step is a couples' class. The teacher is John Thomas who does a great job. The next three weeks he's talking about divorce-proofing our marriages. My wife and I would like to invite you and your wives to meet us for the class and then to lunch with us." Do you see how this is a concrete, believable opportunity that helps a man want to take the next step? Your leaders need to shepherd their men from one step to the next.

The arrows of the *Create-Capture-Sustain* cycle are important! We must develop seamless processes to move men along the continuum.

KEEP THE CONVEYOR BELT MOVING

The belts can't stand still; they need to keep men moving forward in their spiritual journey. Once they have gone through the cycle of *Create-Capture-Sustain*, it will soon be time for another *create* opportunity. A twelve- or eighteen-week small-group study or class semester is great, but that *sustain* activity needs to propel men forward to the next phase of their spiritual growth. Complacent men will get bored and eventually leave.

Incorporate the concept of resonance in your *sustain* activities to help attract men to ongoing spiritual development opportunities. For instance, "Men's Classes" probably doesn't sound very interesting to most men. Simply calling your class "Winners Circle for Men" or "Survival Training" ups the attention it receives. It says, "This is different from the preconception that all classes are boring."

Finally, remember the portal priority. Make sure that all of the ongoing activities you are offering for men are helping them become disciples. Don't let them become places to stick men to keep them busy. Make sure all your efforts are helping achieve the purpose of your men's ministry.

HAVING A LONG-TERM, SUSTAINABLE MEN'S MINISTRY

Perseverance and Patience Required

Manage your expectations and those of your leadership team. Don't expect more than the Bible promises. When you use the *Vision-Create-Capture-Sustain* strategy, expect men to drop away every time you ask for deeper levels of the commitment. Why? It is because the command to make disciples is juxtaposed against the principal sower's parable. In other words, as you go along, some of the seed is snatched away, some withers, and some gets choked by life's riches and worries.

We should not expect a man to hear "the ten things every godly man believes" and completely "get it."

> Some men will need several "cycles" of *create* and *capture* before they're ready for the longer-term spiritual growth of *sustain*. But by the end of each cycle you will also have new men staying involved in your discipleship process.

But don't expect less than the Bible promises either (see John 3:16, 1 Timothy 1:15, Luke 19:10, Matthew 13:24, John 15:9, and John 14:12). The problem is not that our plans are too big, but too small. Raise expectations. Educate leadership (and yourself) about what's really going on. There is a spiritual battle raging for the souls of your men. The secular symptoms we see like crime, divorce, and workaholism are actually results of this spiritual war. God wants us to build Christ's kingdom.

Figure 13 shows the net effect of your ministry—long-term, sustainable growth. Notice the incremental increase in the numbers of disciples over time.

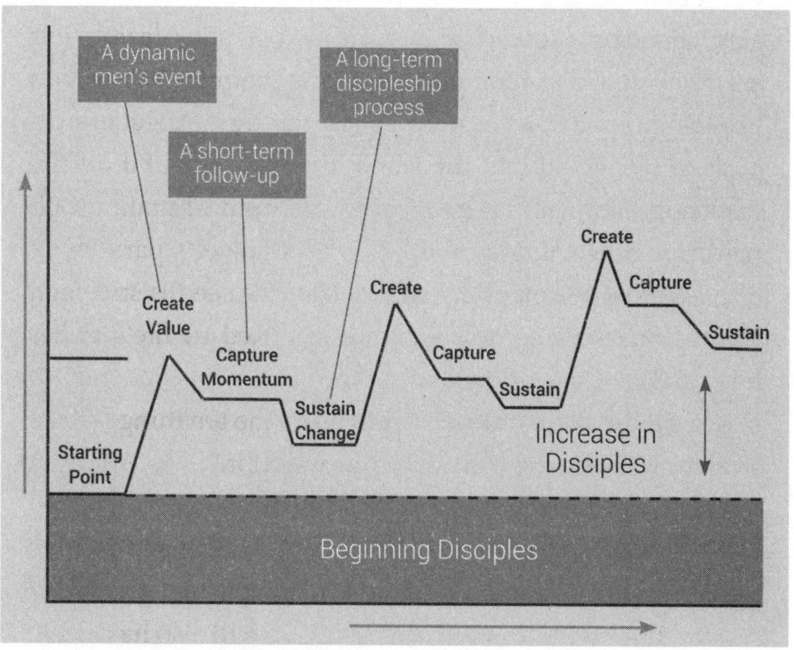

FIGURE 13

The Cumulative Impact of an Ongoing Strategy

Not a Linear Process

Graphs such as Figure 13 make the process seem very neat and orderly. *Create* always leads to *capture* and then to *sustain*. In reality, though, these processes often overlap and intermingle. When a man is young in his spiritual journey, you have to keep creating compelling reasons for him to be involved in the discipleship process. Remember, your ministry to men, and the paths men take toward spiritual maturity, will not be linear.

The *create* step for one man may be the *sustain* step for someone else. For an unchurched guy, being on the softball team last season was a *create* step. He really enjoyed the end-of-season barbecue when he got to meet the priest (a *capture* step). For him, participating in the next season of softball is a *sustain* step. For another man on the softball team, giving his testimony at the need barbecue was a *create* step on his path to leadership. At the same time, one member of the team recruited another member to join his new small group (a *capture* step).

Sustaining momentum is the last step in the system. Now you have a complete picture of the No Man Left Behind Model. But understanding the concepts is not enough to actually make a difference in your parish. So, in chapter twelve we will help you map out what it will look like in your parish.

Remember This . . .

- Two goals for sustaining momentum in your men's ministry are to get men into relationships, and to get men into small groups and the study of Scripture.
- It takes a long time to make a disciple. Don't get angry with men because you are more interested in their spiritual success than they are.
- Rather than showing men a list of "dos" and "don'ts," show them Christ.
- Build everything—your leadership team, your ministry, your discipleship programs and every activity for men—on a foundation of prayer.
- We have never known a man whose life was changed in any significant way without the regular contact with God in his Word and in the sacraments.
- Recruit shepherds—leaders who are eager to show men the love of Christ—not teachers—men who are eager to show off their knowledge.
- Employ the concept of "resonance" in all your *sustain* activities. It's not a "Men's Group" or "Class," it's "Survival Training."
- Your ministry to men, and the paths men take through it toward spiritual maturity, will not be linear. The *Vision-Create-Capture-Sustain* strategy is a mind-set.

Talk About This . . .

1. What activities help you sustain your own spiritual growth? What makes it effective? Great curriculum? Personal discipline? Other men accompanying you on the journey? What else? What does this imply about the other men in your parish?
2. What types of activities appeal the most to you? Ones that appeal to your intellect (head), ones that appeal to your emotions and beliefs (heart), or ones that get you involved in something physical (hands)? Which of these does your parish do the best? The worst?
3. Sometimes a *create* step can be a *sustain* step for someone else. Describe a situation like this in your own ministry.
4. Review the key points at the end of the chapter together and discuss the ones you feel will have the most impact on your ministry.
5. As a team, use the chart on the page 236 to conduct an "audit" of your ministry offerings to men. Start by listing all the ideas and truths that you want a man to have in each area. Put a checkmark next to each item that your parish already provides for men. Circle any items that are not currently available.

Pray About This . . .

Pray together as a leadership team:

- That God will give you wisdom and patience as you seek to draw men closer to him.
- That God would call men together into godly relationships where they will seek him together.
- For men to become hungry for greater contact with God in his Word and in the sacraments.
- For strength on the journey to long-term commitment to forming men as disciples in your parish.

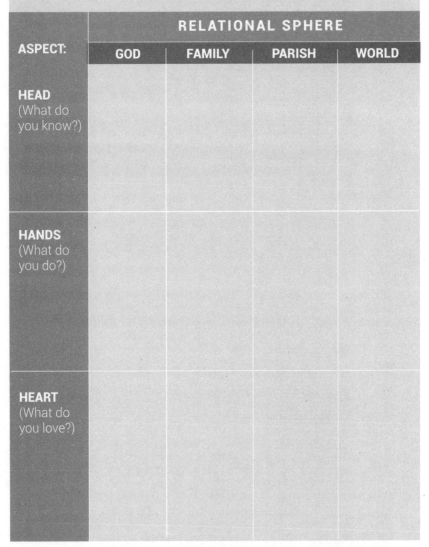

What Should a Disciple Look Like in Your Parish?

If you knew that you were only going to have a man for five years, what are the ideas and experiences that you would want him to get to consider yourself a "success"?

ASPECT:	RELATIONAL SPHERE			
	GOD	FAMILY	PARISH	WORLD
HEAD (What do you know?)				
HANDS (What do you do?)				
HEART (What do you love?)				

Based on a chart developed by the leadership of University Presbyterian Church in Orlando, Florida.

12

BUILD YOUR PLAN: HOW TO IMPLEMENT THE MODEL IN YOUR PARISH

YOU'VE MADE IT! Our goal was that by now you would be so full of ideas that you couldn't wait to get started. Hopefully, you already are.

Before you get too far, though, you might want to picture in your mind what success looks like. Is it a parish full of men who are all involved in a small group? Is it the end of divorce in your parish? Is it a parish calendar full of activities that men can get involved with no matter what their level of spiritual maturity?

"IT'S SOO . . . NATURAL."

Imagine this: A man is being ordained a deacon or commissioned as a lay leader in your parish. His family members are there supporting him, and they are so proud of him—you can see it in their glowing faces. Among those watching are the men who have made an impact on the man's life over the last several years, and men he has impacted as well.

He is asked, "Tell us how God brought you to this point in your spiritual journey."

"To tell you the truth," the man replies, "I'm not really sure. The only decision I can remember making is when my friend invited me to join the softball team ten years ago. After that, it just seemed like every step I took was so . . . well . . . natural. It was like I didn't have to decide what to do next. The right next step just always appeared when I was ready for it."

This notion is similar to being at an airport with those moving walkways. A guy steps on one end, and off he goes to the other end. Sure, he can jump off the side or walk backward, but the system just naturally carries him forward toward the destination.

That's how a discipleship program for men in your parish should work. A man makes a decision to step onto the belt, and off he goes. The program has built-in momentum. And for the man, it's natural.

SO WHAT'S NEXT FOR YOU?

Reading this book has been a *vision* and *create* step for you and your leadership team. The questions in the book and the exercises in this closing chapter will help you *capture* momentum. How well that momentum is *sustained* will be determined by the decisions you make by the end of this chapter, and the actions you take during the next twelve months.

So what comes next? Let's work our way back through the system and map out some next steps to implement the No Man Left Behind Model.

We start with the napkin test exercise. Use this to preview the overall model. Then we focus on the eight components you'll need to build your plan for each concept, and a list of concrete steps or actions is provided to help you implement them in your ministry. We split the activities into short-term—within the next three months—and long-term—within the next year.

We don't want to micromanage you through this (this is only a model of what to do with your men). We also don't want to leave you out in the cold, so here are a couple of ways you could complete your sustainable men's ministry plan.

Eight Sessions

Because this chapter gives you concrete next steps for one sitting or meeting of your leadership team, we suggest you take four sessions to work through the "Within the Next Three Months" activities and four sessions to work through the "Within the Next Year" activities.

If you are meeting with your team on a regular basis, spend your next four meetings on this chapter. (Have each man do the napkin test before your first meeting). Each time, work through two components, completing the "Within the Next Three Months" exercises. After three to six months, have another series of four meetings to complete the "Within the Next Year" activities for each component. This will give you time to actually implement the plans you have made.

Planning Retreat

You could also use a planning retreat for either or both of these sets of activities. Plan to have four sessions during the retreat and cover two of the components during each session. Usually it will be necessary to follow up your retreat with a series of meetings to go over the implementation plans you draft.

During the next year, you will want to refer back to these plans to help you stay on course. As you do these exercises, record your work in a notebook or journal. This will allow you to keep a record of your decisions, as well as facilitate sharing the information with your pastor and new leaders as they join your team.

We've included a handy checklist at the end which gives you a sample schedule. This checklist also makes it easy for you to see if you have completed all the exercises in the chapters.

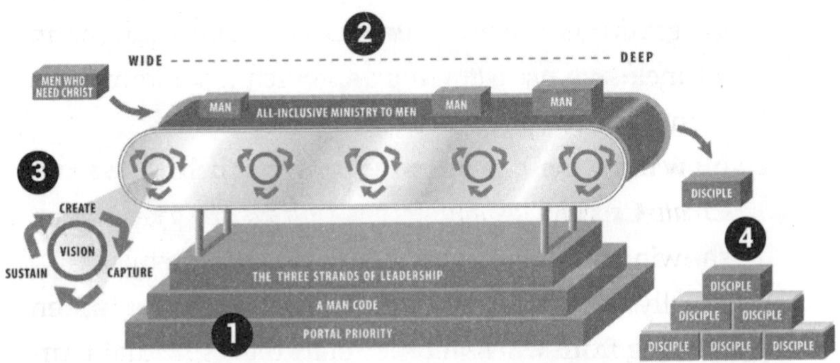

The No Man Left Behind Model

A System Designed to Produce Passionate Disciples

THE NAPKIN TEST

In the introduction, we explained that we wanted to create a model that would pass the napkin test. In other words, could you sit in a coffee shop and explain this model for men's ministry to another man with nothing but a napkin and a pen?

Looking at the illustration on the previous page, here is a quick synopsis of how to explain the model to another man:

1. Start with the three foundations of your ministry. Draw just at the base of your napkin, showing three blocks: the portal priority, man code, and three strands of leadership. Briefly explain each one.
2. Then add the continuum and how it represents the spiritual journey toward becoming a disciple. Draw the conveyor belt with a couple of "man" bricks on it, showing the wide-to-deep continuum. Next, talk about how you're trying to get the men on a conveyor belt moving down this continuum, where every program has an activity in the parish that is part of an all-inclusive ministry to men, which helps move the men forward spiritually.
3. Now draw the engine for the conveyor belt: the *Vision-Create-Capture-Sustain* strategy. Draw the *vision* gear, showing the *create, capture,* and *sustain* components.
4. Finally, show them that the result of the model is men moving from wherever they start their spiritual journey to becoming disciples who help build the parish. Be sure to draw the disciple "bricks" that come off the conveyor belt.

Within the next three months, take a friend to coffee or lunch, grab a napkin, and try it out! Use the space below to practice.

A PLAN FOR THE NEXT YEAR

1. Explaining the Portal Priority

The book began with your philosophy of ministry—discipleship is the portal priority. It is the lens that focuses all the parish's different activities to achieve the outcomes you're seeking (see chapter five). If you don't focus on disciple-making as your portal priority, you'll make donors, singers, and hard workers; not stewards, worshipers, or servants. In short, people will conform to the environment of the parish and exhibit the correct behaviors, but their hearts will not change (see Romans 12:2). External controls have no power to change a man's heart, but discipleship changes men from the inside out.

Here is a picture of the *portal priority.*

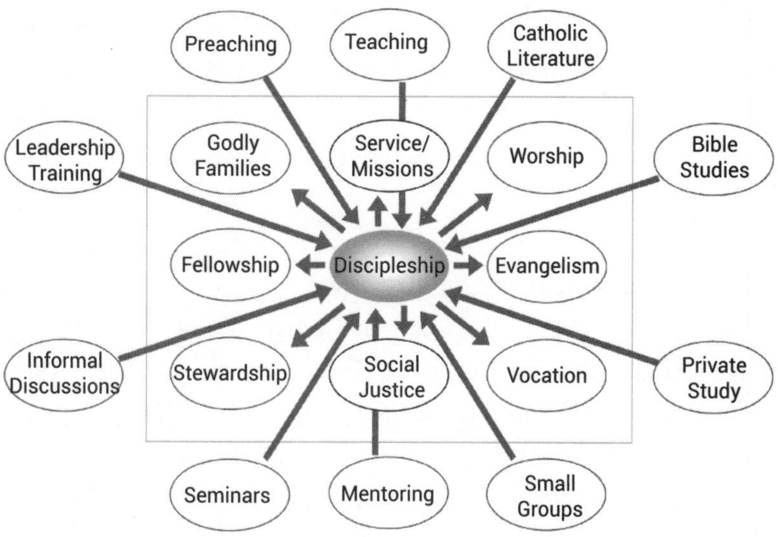

Make a new portal priority chart for your parish. Change the outcomes inside the box to make them match your parish's target outcomes. How does your parish achieve these objectives? Revise the methods (outside the box) and replace with the various activities available to men in your parish. Here's a three- to nine-month plan to do so.

Within the next three months:

- Identify two leaders who represent a disciple-making effort in your parish. These men could include your small groups' leader and a prominent religious education teacher, for example. Engage them in the discussion about the portal priority. Get their reaction to these methods to disciple men and women.

Within the next year:

- Look for an opportunity to share the portal priority with all the leaders in your parish—perhaps on a leadership retreat, at a parish council meeting, or at a staff meeting. You will, of course, need your pastor's buy-in first.

2. *Modifying Your Man Code*

Every man who walks into your parish has an almost instant impression of how your parish regards its men. From the décor to the bulletin to the quality of leadership, men quickly learn what it means to be a man in your parish (see chapter five). How can you help your parish set the right man code for men?

Within the next three months:

- Look around your parish for any obvious decorating that makes men feel welcome. Don't see any? Make some suggestions to the appropriate people about helping men feel more comfortable in your parish. Start with your pastor and go from there. If you are able, offer to pay for the changes. Refer back to your work in chapter five and list some changes you would suggest.

Within the next year:

- Get a group of men together to discuss making the

environment of your parish friendlier to men. Record a few ideas below and pick the best ones to implement. Here are a few samples to get you going:

- Create a men's section in your bulletin. Don't fill it with boring announcements. Have different men write a short testimony for the bulletin once a month. Make it sound challenging and fun to be a man at your parish.
- Put a bulletin board over every urinal in the men's restroom and post your "external challenge" to men, announcements about the men's ministry, along with jokes and the sports page.

What other ideas do you have?

____

____

____

____

____

____

3. *Developing the Three Strands of Leadership*

The cord of three strands is not easily broken. The three strands of leadership for your ministry to men are: your pastor, a passionate leader, and the committed leadership team. (For a detailed discussion, review chapter six.)

Within the next three months:

- Pray for your priests regularly, both individually and with other leaders. Get into the habit of including your pastor in all communications about the men's ministry. Discuss with your leadership team ways you could become known as the pastor's supporters. Write down some specific ways you and your leadership team could be an encouragement to the pastor. (Start here or use a notebook or journal to record your responses.)

- Do you have a passionate leader in your ministry to men? If so, write down his name here (or in your notebook or journal). If not, write down the names of several men who are possibilities. Begin to pray that God would raise up his man.

- Use the two columns (or make them in your notebook or journal). In the first column, list the members of your ministry leadership team. Do they represent the five types of men in your parish whom you are trying to reach? If not, list men in the second column who you might possibly recruit to your leadership team. Within the next three months, get together with one of these men and share your vision for forming men as disciples.

Men on the Ministry Team	Candidates for the Ministry Team

Within the next year:

- Plan a major act of appreciation for your pastor. Have a men's dinner with your pastor as a surprise guest of honor, or find a cabin or retreat he can escape to for a couple of days to get away from it all. Write down some ideas and pick one or two to pursue.

- Do you need to recruit more men for your leadership team? Meet with a different potential leader over coffee or lunch every month for a year. Make it a habit to always be looking for the next man with whom you can share your vision. Get with your leadership team to make a list of men whose active involvement you will seek.

____

____

____

____

- Your leadership team must become to each other what they hope the men of the parish will become. There are lots of Catholic materials available—The Dynamic Catholic Institute is a good place to start.

4. Developing an All-Inclusive Ministry to Men

Everything your parish does that touches men is men's ministry, even if it's not a men's-only program. Your men's ministry is made up of every man in your parish, plus the men you'd like to be there. (For a detailed discussion, review chapter seven.) Also look for opportunities for the men's ministry to support the other ministries of the parish. Additionally, look for ways to connect more men to the different initiatives that are working to disciple men in your parish.

Within the next three months:

- List some existing ministries in your parish not traditionally considered "men's ministries." What are concrete ways you could help them reach men more effectively?

Within the next year:

- Help every man in your parish come to the realization that he is part of your men's ministry. How can you achieve that? List eight or ten major ways that men are involved in your parish, and beside each one, write down one or two concrete steps to help them feel a part of what God is doing through the men in your parish.

Example:
Men working in the soup kitchen.
Give them aprons with the men's ministry logo.
Men helping in youth sports league.
Have an appreciation dinner for coaches and referees.

5. Clarifying your vision

Help men answer the question, "Why are we doing this?" Everyone wants to feel as though they're making a contribution; they want to know they're achieving something. A ministry that is just a series of disconnected activities will soon run out of steam.

In chapter eight, you worked on an internal purpose statement, an external slogan, and an elevator speech. Having a clear vision helps you focus your energy to achieve worthy goals:

- Your internal purpose statement helps your leadership team decide what you will and won't do.
- Your external slogan needs to resonate with men, calling them to be a part of something bigger than themselves.
- The elevator speech explains your vision for men in a few short sentences, and is particularly helpful in recruiting new leaders.

Within the next three months:

- Develop an external slogan for your men's ministry efforts. Write down some ideas here (or in your notebook or journal), and work on it as a team. Get the acceptance and support of your pastor and other leaders.

____

____

____

____

Within the next year:

- Develop a new internal purpose statement for your men's ministry. Don't forget, your purpose statement is dynamic. It can change from year to year as your objectives change. But make sure your purpose statement is in line with the mission of the parish. Refer to the work you did in chapter eight and write a draft statement below. Get more men involved in reviewing and agreeing on these priorities.

____

____

____

____

- Help each man in your leadership team develop an elevator speech—three to five sentences that explain your vision for the men of the parish. You could start with your draft from chapter eight and get feedback from other men. Then distribute your final draft to other leaders and ask them to personalize the speech for their own use with men.

6. Creating Value

We create momentum by attracting men to go to the next level. We do this by providing something of value to them. For guys at the beginning of their journey, value may come from fun and fellowship. But as a man moves forward, he should have his spiritual needs met more directly.

Note: For the *create* and *capture* exercises below, be sure to refer back to the work you did in the "Talk About This" discussion questions at the end of chapters nine and ten.

Within the next three months:

- Do you have any events planned in the near future? Write them down below. Then indicate which of the five types of men each event will focus on, and how you will personally invite men to attend. What might you change about these events based on what you have read?

____

____

____

____

____

____

Within the next year:

- Use separate paper or spreadsheets to plan out a twelve-month calendar for creating opportunities for the men of your parish. (Remember, these do not have to be men's-only initiatives, and, as we've said elsewhere, they don't even have to be planned by your leadership team.) Try and make sure there is at least one opportunity for each type of man in your parish during the year. Also make sure that your activities support the men's ministry's overall purpose.

7. Capturing Momentum

There is no point in giving men any kind of emotional or spiritual high without giving them the right next step they need to maintain the ground they've gained. Never create momentum—whether it's a big event or lunch with a new man—without a plan for what's next. Adopt the "right next step" mind-set to avoid wasted efforts. The right next step is always concrete and achievable—a man leaves already having made the commitment and knowing what he will do next.

Within the next three months:

- Look at the events and opportunities you already have scheduled for men. Does each activity have a clear and appropriate next step for men who will participate? Refer to your list above and write down what the next step will be for each activity or event occurring in the next six months. Begin to build a chart that shows "pathways" through your men's discipleship programs. See the examples below, and use the chart at the end of the chapter.

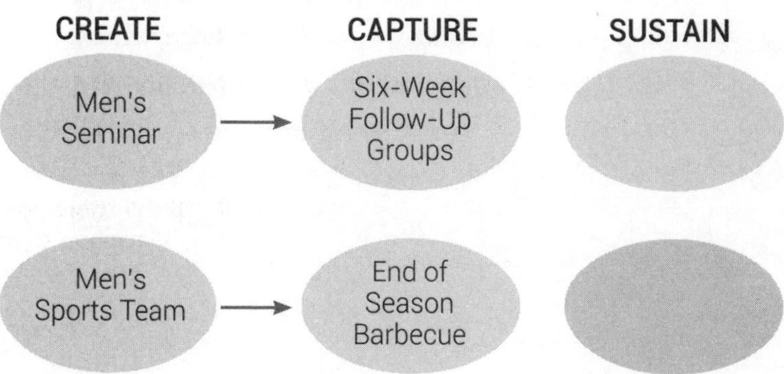

Note: It is impossible to have more than one *capture* opportunity for a *create* activity. For instance, if you are creating momentum for a leader by having coffee with him to discuss your vision for forming men as disciples, you may invite him to pray for some specific needs and how he might want to get involved, invite him to your next leadership team meeting, or, based on his interest, invite him to a small group leaders training class. All of those would be suitable *capture* steps, but there cannot be more than one per momentum-building activity.

Within the next year:

- Adopt the "right next step" mind-set in all of your interactions with men. Now that you've learned this technique of charting your activities, each time you plan an activity of any type, draw a "pathway" for a man who attends that shows what the *capture* step will be. Assign each activity to a leader who will ensure that these follow-up steps are executed.

8. Sustain Momentum

Long-term change almost always happens in the context of relationships. How will you engage men in relationship-based discipleship opportunities in the parish? Sustain change in men's lives by focusing on their spiritual lives, not their behavior (review chapter eleven). Do not allow men to look good on the outside but be hollow and dead on the inside. Challenge men's motivations more than their behavior.

Within the next three months:

- Make a list of the different ongoing discipleship opportunities in your parish according to the five types of men described in chapter eleven. For example, include adult faith formation classes, small groups, and service opportunities.

MEN WHO NEED CHRIST

____

____

____

____

UNENGAGED CATHOLIC MEN

____

____

____

____

MATURE CATHOLIC MEN

____

____

____

____

LEADERS OF CATHOLIC MEN

____

____

____

____

MEN WHO ARE HURTING

____

____

____

____

- How will you plug men into these activities? Use the chart at the end of the chapter to map how you will connect men at the *capture* step to the ongoing discipleship opportunities listed above. Here's an example of a "completed" pathway:

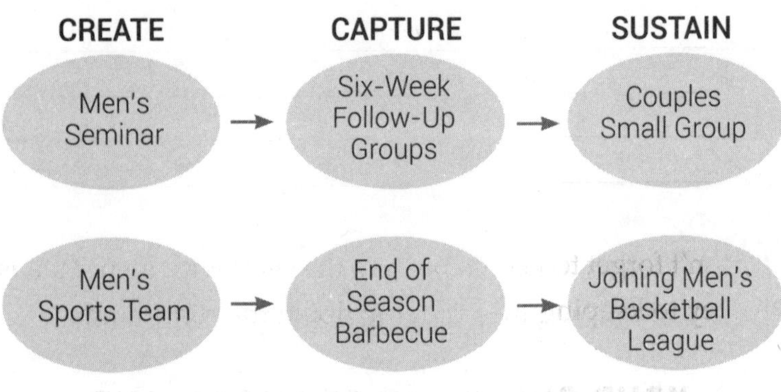

Note: There can be multiple *sustain* opportunities after a *capture* step. For instance, you may offer the men in the six-week follow-up groups a choice between staying in their groups for another six or twelve weeks, joining a couples small group with their wives, or joining a regular faith formation class. Remember that the leader of the *capture* step is personally responsible for shepherding men into the *sustain* activity.

Within the next year:

- Refer back to your head-heart-hands chart from chapter eleven. Do you see any holes in the current offerings of the parish for men? Plan to develop new longer-term discipleship opportunities for men that fill these gaps. These will need to be implemented over the next several years. Make a list below of two or three different *sustain* opportunities not currently available that you would like to offer men. Begin praying about the steps you will need to take to make these a reality.

____

____

____

____

Don't forget to keep repeating the cycle with men. That is the key to keeping men moving down the continuum.

YOUR CHECKLIST OF SHORT- AND LONG-TERM ACTIVITIES

Here's a checklist of the short- and long-term activities compiled from above.

Within the Next Three Months

Session One:

☐ Do the "napkin test" with a friend.

- ☐ Discuss the portal priority with two disciple-making leaders in your parish. For instance, the small group leader and the director of religious education.
- ☐ Compile a list of subtle decorating changes that would make your parish more welcoming to men.
- ☐ Discuss it with your pastor.

Session Two:

- ☐ Make it a habit to pray for your priests regularly, both individually and with leaders.
- ☐ Make a list of specific ways you could be an encouragement to the priests in your parish.
- ☐ If you don't have an overall men's ministry leader, make a list of men passionate about discipleship, and pray that God will call his man to lead your ministry.
- ☐ Make a list of men on your leadership team. Make a second list of men you might want to recruit to your team to help you reach the five types of men described in chapter eleven.
- ☐ Make a list of existing ministries in your parish not traditionally considered men's ministries. Look for concrete ways to help them reach men more effectively.

Session Three:

- ☐ Develop an external slogan for your men's ministry efforts.
- ☐ For upcoming *create* events, determine which of the five types of men the event will target and how men will be personally invited to the event.

Session Four:

- ☐ Determine the *capture* step for each *create* event you listed, and begin a chart that shows the "pathways" men will follow.
- ☐ Make a list of the different ongoing discipleship opportunities of your parish, organized according to the five types of men (*sustain*).
- ☐ For each *create-capture* pathway, chart the potential *sustain* step that a man could take at the end of the *capture* step.

Within the Next Year

Session One:

- ☐ Share the portal priority with all the leaders of your parish.
- ☐ Gather a group of men to discuss making your parish environment friendlier to men, from the decor to the bulletin to the liturgy. Start implementing a few ideas.

Session Two:

- ☐ Plan a major act of appreciation for your priests. Be creative.
- ☐ Share your vision for forming men as disciples with a different potential leader every month. Get members of your leadership team to commit to doing this as well.
- ☐ Start a discipleship curriculum with your leadership team.
- ☐ Make a list of ways men are involved in your par-

ish. Design concrete steps to make those men feel involved in what God is doing through the men in your parish.

Session Three:

- ☐ Develop a new internal purpose statement.
- ☐ Help each man on the leadership team develop his elevator speech.
- ☐ Create a twelve-month calendar for *create* opportunities. Start with activities already planned by your parish that men can participate in, then add men's-only events to ensure that all five types of men will be reached at least once.

Session Four:

- ☐ Determine the *capture* step for every *create* opportunity in your calendar—even those that are not for men only. Chart the *create-capture* sequences to build pathways men will follow.
- ☐ For each *create-capture* pathway, chart the potential *sustain* step that a man could take at the end of the *capture* step.
- ☐ Using the head-heart-hands chart, look for "gaps" in your parish's current ongoing discipleship opportunities for men. Make long-term plans to develop *sustain*-type opportunities to fill those gaps.

Use the chart below (or make your own) to map out "pathways" for men through your discipleship programs.

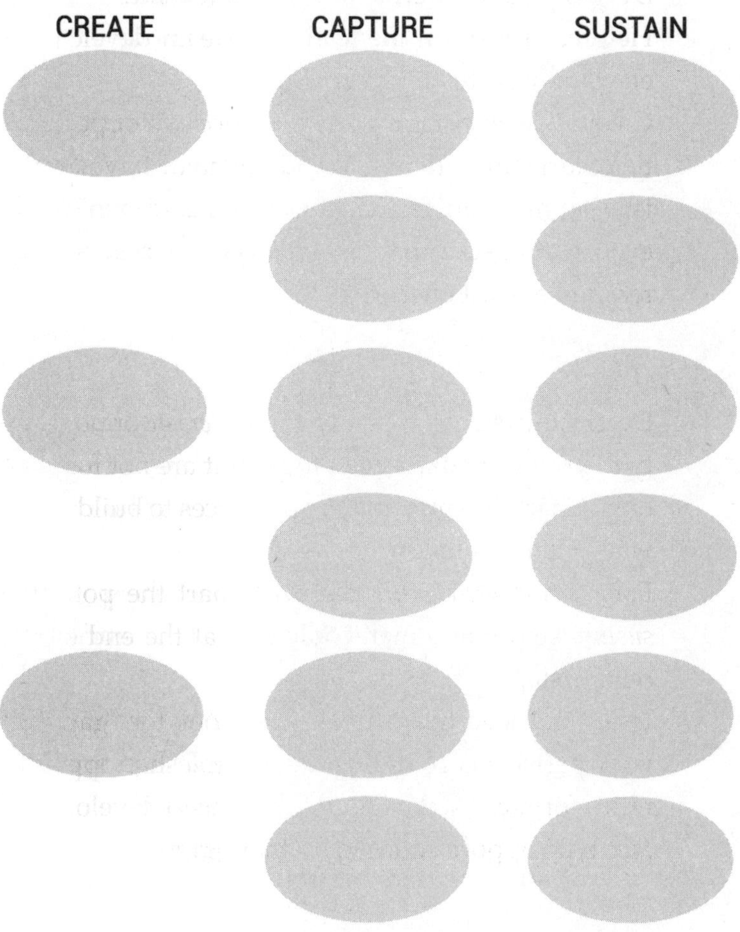

EPILOGUE: RAISING UP FOURTH-SEED LEADERS

IN THE PARABLE of the sower and the seed, Jesus described four seeds. Of the fourth seed, he said, "As for what was sown on good soil, this is he who hears the word and understands it; he indeed bears fruit, and yields, in one case a hundredfold, in another sixty, and in another thirty" (Matthew 13:23). We call this type of man a "fourth-seed leader."

A fourth-seed leader is a person who "gets" the gospel, increasingly feels humbled by the grace of God, and lives in the overflow of a vibrant relationship with Jesus Christ. The fourth-seed leaders feel like they will explode unless they can lead others to a deeper relationship with Christ and help them grow.

Fourth-seed leaders must share the gospel or they cannot be happy. They want to "bear much fruit, and so prove to be [Christ's] disciples" (John 15:8). Isn't this the type of leader you want to be? Aren't these the kind of leaders you want to develop?

WHERE ARE THE FOURTH-SEED LEADERS?

According to www.cara.georgetown.edu, as of 2016 there were 17,233 Roman Catholic parishes. Approximately seven million men age fifteen and older are in these parishes. We estimate that 1 percent of all American Catholic men are fourth-seed leaders—leaders passionate about reaching men for Jesus Christ. That would be an average of about four men per parish. Many women also are passionate about seeing men find faith.

NEEDED: MORE FOURTH-SEED LEADERS

Some leaders are content reaching a circle of three, six, or even ten people. Let's applaud this—better six walking a close relationship with Christ then zero. But to achieve Christ's vision to make disciples of every willing man, woman, and child, we also need leaders who dream big, think big, risk big. Are you a leader who wants to reach your entire parish, your whole diocese, your whole city, all your peers? Are you a leader who wants to reach thirty, sixty, or a hundred or more souls for Jesus Christ? Are you committed to the vision that no Catholic man will be left behind? Would you like to see God do something great through your life? If so, welcome to the battle for men's souls—you are a fourth-seed leader.

Our prayer is that this book has equipped you to implement a discipleship system in your parish and multiply yourself like the fourth seed in Jesus' parable. We pray it also helps you raise up other leaders to join you.

WHY "NO MAN LEFT BEHIND"?

God has given us the responsibility and privilege of spiritual leadership. He has called us to disciple every man in our parishes and dioceses. The consequences are too important for us not to do our absolute best to be faithful.

Above all else, leadership is a calling—a calling from God. Your life and ministry can be a spiritual outpost for men—a new rescue mission, a halfway house, a hospital for men with broken wings. We are here to help men change the core affections of their hearts, to help them believe that the gospel can change their lives, to show them a living (though imperfect) example of a man after God's own heart.

Jesus entrusts men to us. He said:

> "Now after a long time the master of those servants came and settled accounts with them. And he who had received the five talents came forward, bringing five talents more, saying 'Master, you delivered to me five talents; here I have made five more.' His master said to him, 'Well done, good and faithful servant; you have been faithful over a little, I will set you over much; enter into the joy of your master.'" (Matthew 25:19–21)

We are not responsible for the outcomes with our men, but we are responsible to be faithful to them.

Responsibility requires commitment. "Not many of you should be presumed to be teachers, my brothers, because you know that we who teach will be judged more strictly" (James 3:1). We remind ourselves that the stakes are high.

This also requires a team effort. If you read this book by yourself, begin to pray about other men whom God might call to join you in your efforts to disciple men. As you will see, no leader can do this on his own.

To lead men is also a rare and holy privilege; we get to join God himself in his work. All around us a battle rages for men's souls. God is with us in the battle; together we can win. We cannot, we must not, and by God's grace, we will not fail!

Therefore, let us pledge to be found faithful.

God, we pray for the strength, wisdom, and time to produce a crop—a hundred, sixty, or thirty times what you have sown into us. Help us to faithfully discharge the responsibilities of forming men as disciples to which we now pledge ourselves. And may you use this book in the lives of leaders to ensure that no Catholic man is left behind. In Jesus' name we pray. Amen.

Are you a fourth-seed leader? Would you like to connect with other leaders like you for encouragement, to share ideas, and to learn best practices? Send an email to nfcmusa.com for information about how to join the leadership community. You'll get access to two online resources for Catholic men's ministry leadership.

THE BIG IDEAS

We've collected the Big Ideas from each chapter into one page to help you review the major concepts of the No Man Left Behind Model. (This should help you pass the napkin test!)

1. The discipleship system of your church is perfectly designed to produce the kind of men you have sitting in the pews.
2. A spiritual reformation of society starts with a spiritual reformation of men.
3. A disciple is called to walk with Christ, equipped to live like Christ, and sent to work for Christ. *(Disciple)*
4. Christianity is not about behavior modification; it's about spiritual transformation.
5. Within a few weeks, a man understands what it means to be a man in your parish. *(Man Code)*
6. The three strands of leadership for your ministry are the priest, a primary leader, and a leadership team. *(The Three Strands of Leadership)*

7. Build a seamless process to move men across the wide-to-deep continuum.
8. An all-inclusive men's ministry maximizes the impact of every interaction with every man, no matter the setting. *(An All-Inclusive Ministry to Men)*
9. Ideas are more powerful than labor. Ideas set forces in motion that, once released, can no longer be contained. *(Vision)*
10. Give men what they need in the context of what they want. *(Create)*
11. Whenever you create momentum, always show men a right next step. *(Capture)*
12. We have never known a man whose life has changed in any significant way apart from regular contact with God in his Word and in the sacraments. *(Sustain)*

NOTES

1. United States Conference of Catholic Bishops (USCCB), *Our Hearts Were Burning Within Us: A Pastoral Plan for Adult Faith Formation in the United States* (1999).
2. USCCB, *Catholic Men's Ministries: A Progress Report by the Committee on Marriage and Family and the Committee on Evangelization* (2002).
3. Pope John Paul II, *L'Osservatore Romano* (March 24, 1993), p. 3.
4. Richard J. Foster, *Celebration of Discipline: The Path to Spiritual Growth* (Grand Rapids, Mich.: Zondervan, 1988) p. 107.
5. http://cara.georgetown.edu/frequently-requested-church-statistics/.
6. USCCB, *Our Hearts Were Burning within Us: A Pastoral Plan for Adult Faith Formation in the United States* (November 17, 1999).
7. The National Fellowship of Catholic Men offers these types of resources on its website at nfcmusa.com.
8. U.S. Census Bureau; Wade F. Horn and Tom Sylvester, *Father Facts* (Gaithersburg, Md.: National Fatherhood Initiative, 2002).
9. http://nineteensixtyfour.blogspot.com/2013/09/divorce-still-less-likely-among.html.
10. James Dobson, *Bringing Up Boys* (Wheaton, III: Tyndale, 2001), p. 160.
11. "Swim with the Sharks (and Survive)," *Go Magazine*.
12. Ralph Mattson and Arthur Miller, *Finding A Job You Can*

Love (Nashville: Thomas Nelson, 1982), p. 123.

13. http://www.covenanteyes.com/pornstats/ (2014).
14. The article appeared in the December 10, 2004, issue of the *Washington Post*, and is cited with permission.
15. Pope Paul VI, *Evangelization in the Modern World* (Vatican City: Libreria Editrice Vaticana, 1975), 14.
16. Ibid., 27.
17. John Paul II, *Ecclesia de Eucharistia* (Vatican City: Libreria Editrice Vaticana, 2003).

APPENDIX A

Twenty-Five Ways to Connect with Your Pastors and Priests

If we want to connect with our priests, the overarching idea is to not put demands on them. Instead, help them accomplish their mission. In a way, we become a part of their ministry instead of the object of their ministry. Here are twenty-five additional ideas:

DO

1. Write your priest a note affirming a job well done. Think of something very specific he does well, e.g., his homilies or the way he listens in confession.
2. Invite your neighbors to church and introduce them to your priest after Mass.
3. Tell the priests in your parish you are praying for them—and then do it. If you are close enough, ask for specific prayer requests.
4. Always speak well of your priests. Little birds inevitably chirp when you say bad things.
5. Always defend your pastor. The principle is, "I stick up for my friends."
6. Ask your pastor what his goals are and how you can help him.
7. Volunteer to serve in the parish.
8. Present your parish priest a gift card to his favorite restaurant.
9. Ask to start a small group to disciple some of the men in

the parish—better yet, just do it.

10. Ask for your priests' opinions about which discipleship materials you should use.
11. Be a just and godly man, husband, and father yourself. Be a blessing rather than a burden to your priests.
12. Be a good financial steward; tithe.
13. Participate in a small group.
14. Pray with your wife. (This will reduce your pastor's counseling load.)
15. Read the Scriptures every day. Fill up with the Word of God—this can't help but overflow in ways visible to others (although probably not to you).
16. Take your children to Mass and religious ed. Godly children are a blessing in any parish. (If it is important to you, it will be important to them.)

DON'T

1. Don't expect your priests to attend too many social events. Instead express your love and appreciation verbally—or better yet, send a handwritten note. Respect the fact that time is a parish priest's most limited resource.
2. Don't offer constructive criticism until you have earned the right (ten praises before you even come close to qualifying for one constructive criticism).
3. Don't criticize your priests behind their backs. If you like what's going on, tell your friends. If you don't like what's going on, tell your pastor (but refer to previous "don't").
4. Don't expect your priests to be televangelists or EWTN personalities.

5. Don't put pressure on your pastor to put resources into your program. Instead, just start forming men as disciples and, as your ministry grows, tell or send your pastor success stories. Results first, then support follows in its proper order.
6. Don't be angry with your priests for merely being human.
7. Don't put pressure on priests that will strain their mental and physical health.

Adapted from *The Weekly Briefing* by Patrick Morley, volume 126. Available online at www.maninthemirror.org.

APPENDIX B

Sample Vision Statements

The following vision components—internal purpose statements, external slogans, and ministry names—were submitted by various churches with whom Man in the Mirror has worked. We appreciate their willingness to share them.

Internal Purpose Statements

1. The purpose of Iron Man Men's Ministry is to help the men of our church become disciples—men who were called to walk with Christ, equipped to live like Christ, and sent to work for Christ (2 Timothy 3:15–17). We will do this by helping men develop authentic relationships with Christian men that will help them:

- Find the true meaning of the gospel, true relevant teaching, and shared experiences;
- Become leaders in their households and in their church; and
- Be living examples of the gospel in the marketplace, the community, and the world.

2. Developing godly men and leaders, through training on the practical, day-to-day applications of the Word of God and through service to meet the various needs of the community.

3. Growing godly men through relational discipleship and the power of the Holy Spirit.

4. To build relationships with men, to encourage them practically, and bring them closer to Christ through fellowship, mentoring, and discipling.

5. To become a community of transformed men who leave a lasting legacy to the honor of Jesus Christ.

6. To encourage and equip (form) every man to be committed, competent, creative, and compassionate in serving others for the glory of God.

7. The purpose of our men's ministry is to:

- Help connect men into deeper relationships with other Christian men who encourage, support, and pray for each other in their struggles against all types of sin. "Iron sharpens iron, and one man sharpens another" (Proverbs 27:17).
- Help men start or continue their journey toward becoming an authentic Christian man who follows Jesus. "Go therefore and make disciples of all nations, baptizing them in the name of the Father, and of the Son, and of the Holy Spirit" (Matthew 28:19).
- Equip (form) men for spiritual service in the home, workplace, and community while finding proper balance for their commitments to family, work, and faith. "If they hearken and serve him, they complete their days in prosperity, and their years in pleasantness" (Job 36:11).

External Slogans

- Sharpening Men to Transform the World
- Brothers in the Great Adventure
- Training Men for the Battle
- First In . . . Last Out . . . No Man Left Behind!
- Changing Men's Hearts One at a Time
- His Work in Progress
- Transforming Our Community, One Man at a Time
- ADAPT (Accountability, Discipleship, and Prayer Together)
- Preparing Men—Proclaiming Christ

Ministries' Names

- Iron Men (or Iron Man)
- Band of Brothers
- Fishers of Men
- Men of A.I.M. (Action, Integrity, Maturity)
- First Pursuit
- Men of Adventure
- Journeymen

APPENDIX C

Creating Momentum for the Five Types of Men

(Forty ideas across the continuum)

WIDE - DEEP

Type 1: **Need Christ**	Type 2: **Unengaged**	Type 3: **Mature Catholics**	Type 4: **Leaders**	Type 5: **Hurting Men**
Softball team	Daily Mass and reception of the Eucharist	Daily Mass and reception of the Eucharist	Leadership training	Daily Mass and reception of the Eucharist
Basketball league	Reconciliation	Reconciliation	Small group leaders workshop	Reconciliation
Hunting or fishing	Adoration	Adoration	Spiritual direction	Adoration
Adventure trip (one-day)	Rosary group	Scripture meditation	Off-site conferences, retreats, and leadership seminars (diocesan, regional, national)	Scripture meditation
Classic car club	Stations of the Cross	Rosary group		Rosary group
Car care day for single moms	Men's seminar	Stations of the Cross		Stations of the Cross
Daddy-daughter dance	Financial seminar	Small group		Grief support groups
Sporting events	Parish picnic	Bible study		Financial seminars
Paintball	Service project	Adult faith formation		Parenting a difficult child classes
Job fair	Adventure retreat	Men's retreat		Divorce recovery group
Go-kart racing	Men's conference	Mission trip		Sexual addictions group/counseling
	Knights of Columbus informational meeting	Ongoing service opportunity		Marriage support group
		Rite of passage for youth		Curriculum for purity
		Men's conference		

NOTE: Remember that men who are hurting can be found in each of the above categories. Therefore, when you take care of the first four types of men, you will minister to this fifth type as well.

APPENDIX D

Vision, Mission & Strategy

Our Vision

A Network of Catholic Men's Fellowships United in Impacting the World for Christ & His Church

Our Mission

1. To evangelize, assist, and provide every Catholic diocese a proven, easily implemented local Catholic Men's ministry
2. To identify and recommend orthodox Catholic apostolate resources of benefit to existing fellowship leaders in their local efforts to evangelize, form, and mobilize men
3. To provide shared technology solutions, leadership training, and other services for fellowships that would be difficult for a local fellowship to create, fund, and maintain

Our Strategies

Evangelize Catholic men to Jesus Christ and root them in the Catholic Church by providing a structure that:

- Builds awareness through the use of national Catholic media of existing fellowships and offer newly interested dioceses supportive services and programs
- Assists local lay Catholic men's ministry leaders in developing and equipping fellowship groups, conferences, and other evangelistic activities
- Works with bishops, pastors, and other ecclesial leaders in the development and provision of Catholic men's formation processes
- Collaborates with other orthodox Catholic organizations, apostolates, and ministries in supporting Catholic men
- Assists Catholic men's experience of local, national, and global community by leveraging technology
- Provides lay Catholic men's leadership training, workshops, and retreats

NOTES

NOTES